Ideal for the
rt Course
;CSE RE

001150

Thinking Through Religion

Teacher's Resource File

Chris Wright

Carrie Mercier

Richard Bromley

David Worden

OXFORD

OXFORD

UNIVERSITY PRESS

Great Clarendon Street, Oxford OX2 6DP

Oxford University Press is a department of the University of Oxford. It furthers the University's objective of excellence in research, scholarship, and education by publishing worldwide in

Oxford   New York

Athens   Auckland   Bangkok   Bogotá   Buenos Aires
Calcutta   Cape Town   Chennai   Dar es Salaam   Delhi
Florence   Hong Kong   Istanbul   Karachi
Kuala Lumpur   Madrid   Melbourne   Mexico City
Mumbai   Nairobi   Paris   São Paulo   Singapore
Shanghai   Taipei   Tokyo   Toronto   Warsaw

with associated companies in Berlin   Ibadan

Oxford is a registered trade mark of Oxford University Press in the UK and in certain other countries

© C Wright, C Mercier, R Bromley, D Worden 2000

Database right Oxford University Press (maker)

First published 2000
Reprinted 2001

ISBN 0 19 917258 7

A CIP catalogue record for this book is available from the British Library.

Printed by Athenæum Press, Great Britain.

The Authors and Publisher are grateful to the following for their permission to reproduce copyright material as credited on the pages in question: Professor E.J. Burge and the *Church Times*: 'Today's Story of Creation', page 87; *The Daily Mail*/Solo Syndication: page 73; *The Daily Telegraph*: pages 44 and 45; The M. K. Gandhi Institute for Nonviolence (interview from *San Jose Mercury News*): pages 31-32; *The Guardian*: page 107; the Alistair Hardy Society, Westminster College, Oxford: pages 54 and 55; *Hinduism Today*, 107 Kaholalele Road, Kapaa, HI, 96746 USA: page 30; *The Independent*: pages 70, 75 and 76, 95; Islamic Relief: page 102; *Jerusalem Post*: page 40; Lutterworth Press: page 106; McGraw Hill: page 111; Souvenir Press: pages 71, 74; Trentham Books Ltd: page 41. Special thanks are due to Preet Mohan S. Ahluwalia for his help in providing material on Sikhism.

The Authors and Publisher are also grateful for permission to reproduce extracts from various publications as annotated in the text. Every effort has been made to reach copyright holders, but the Publisher will make amendments at the next reprint, if necessary.

Contents

The aims of *Thinking Through Religion*

This *Teacher's Resource File* accompanies the student textbook entitled *Thinking Through Religion*. The aims of the *Thinking Through Religion* course are:

1) To meet the requirements of the National Criteria in Religious Education

The QCA Criteria for a GCSE Short Course in Religious Education state that students should:

- acquire and develop knowledge and develop understanding of the beliefs, values, and traditions of one or more religions;
- consider the influence of the beliefs, values, and traditions associated with one or more religions;
- consider religious and other responses to moral issues;
- identify, investigate, and respond to fundamental questions of life raised by religion and human experience.

The *Thinking Through Religion* student textbook and this *Teacher's Resource File* have been designed to meet the needs of teachers providing courses to satisfy statutory requirements for RE at Key Stage 4. We have taken account of the content and approaches of all of the Short Course examination syllabuses. (See the Syllabus Grid on page 6.)

2) To contribute to students' spiritual, moral, social, and cultural development

Through its rich collection of spiritual stories and its many probing questions, *Thinking Through Religion* encourages students' spiritual, moral, social, and cultural development. Students using the course are asked to reflect on their own views about the issues studied. *Thinking Through Religion* avoids presenting religious material as merely facts to be learned for an examination. The course leads students to learn *from* religion as well as *about* religion. The focus of the course is the students' own quest in thinking through religion.

3) To explore important questions of meaning

Where did the universe come from? Does God exist? Why is there so much suffering? Is there a life after death? As teachers we are faced with students asking questions like these every day. Such questions are immediately interesting and relevant. They are at the core of the religious quest. *Thinking Through Religion* allows students to consider these important questions and to learn from the insights of six of the principal world faiths. Students are encouraged to offer their own response at each stage of the process.

4) To explore questions of meaning and contemporary moral issues within the context of six world religions

One of the strengths of this course is that it provides a rich resource of material for understanding the perspectives of Christianity, Buddhism, Hinduism, Islam, Judaism, and Sikhism. Part A of *Thinking Through Religion* provides a summary of the key beliefs, teachings, concepts, and practices of each of these religions. In each chapter of Parts B and C of the course, there are Religion Files on the six religions. These files present the core teachings of the religions on questions of meaning and contemporary moral issues.

How to use *Thinking Through Religion*

Part A: Believing

Includes 6 chapters exploring the beliefs and practices of Christianity, Buddhism, Hinduism, Islam, Judaism, and Sikhism.

Chapters are divided into Units.
An introduction to each unit tells students what they will learn and
think about.

The main text provides a comprehensive overview. It provides enough information for high achievers but is accessible to all the ability range.

Quotations from scriptures, religious thinkers, individual followers of the faiths, and others give a wide range of perspectives.

Questions throughout the book engage students in reflection and help them to recall, select, explain, and evaluate the material studied.

Part B: Questioning

Includes 7 chapters providing information and provoking thought on questions of meaning and contemporary issues.

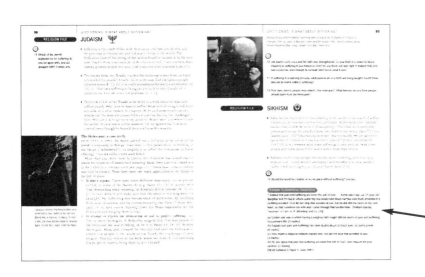

Information Files provide key definitions and facts.

Part C: Acting

Includes 6 chapters investigating how beliefs affect the way people live, as individuals and in society.

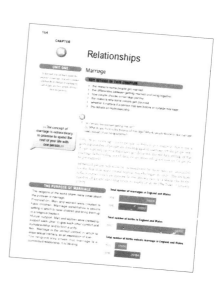

Stories from all the religions studied encourage students to reflect on the spiritual issues at the heart of each topic.

Each chapter in Parts B and C ends with six Religion Files providing succinct information about how religious teachings are applied to the questions under discussion.

Examination Questions from past papers of several examination boards are provided at the end of each chapter in Parts B and C.

Syllabus Grid

Thinking Through Religion meets the needs of all examination syllabuses, as this chart shows.

Thinking Through Religion chapter	Resource File Activity Sheet	OCR Syllabus A	OCR Syllabus B	NEAB Syllabus A	NEAB Syllabus D	SEG	ULEAC Syllabus A	ULEAC Syllabus B	WJEC
Introduction (ways of making moral decisions)	Intro. 1 – Intro. 4	*							
1 Christianity	1. 1 – 1. 7	*		*		*		*	
2 Buddhism	2. 1 – 2. 4	*		*		*		*	
3 Hinduism	3. 1 – 3. 3	*		*		*		*	
4 Islam	4. 1 – 4. 4	*		*		*		*	
5 Judaism	5. 1 – 5. 3	*		*		*		*	
6 Sikhism	6. 1 – 6. 4	*		*		*		*	
7 Does God exist? (nature of God)	7. 1 – 7. 6		*		*	*	*		*
8 Suffering	8. 1 – 8. 4		*		*	*	*		
9 Life after death	9. 1 – 9. 4	*	*			*	*		*
10 Abortion	10. 1 – 10. 3	*	*	*	*	*	*		
11 Euthanasia	11. 1 – 11. 3	*	*	*	*	*	*		*
12 War and peace	12. 1 – 12. 4	*	*		*	*		*	
13 Planet Earth	13. 1 – 13. 6		*	*	*	*	*		*
14 Relationships	14. 1 – 14. 7	*	*	*	*	*	*		*
15 Wealth/poverty	15. 1 – 15. 4		*	*	*	*	*		
16 Prejudice	16. 1 – 16. 3	*	*	*	*	*	*	*	*
17 Work/leisure	17. 1 – 17. 4		*			*			
18 Religion/Science	18. 1 – 18. 2		*			*			
19 Religion/arts/media	19. 1 – 19. 4					*	*		

How to use this *Teacher's Resource File*

This *Teacher's Resource File* is a supplement to the student textbook *Thinking Through Religion*. It contains pages of Teacher's Information; Activity Sheets; Study Skills Sheets; and a list of Useful Addresses. You will find a Teacher's Information page, several Activity Sheets, and a Study Skills Sheet to go with each chapter of the student textbook.

Teacher's Information pages

These pages provide (a) a clear overview of the key issues covered in the chapter, and (b) an introduction to the Activity Sheets and Study Skills Sheet which relate to the chapter.

Activity Sheets

Several Activity Sheets are provided for use alongside each chapter of *Thinking Through Religion*. The sheets serve a number of purposes: (a) they are useful for homework; (b) they contain valuable extension material for the more able; (c) they provide opportunities for revision of topics.

Study Skills Sheets

Two Study Skills Sheets at the beginning of this *Resource File* (pages 8 and 9) provide general advice. Other Study Skills Sheets throughout the book (for instance on pages 56-57) contain examples of answers to past SEG examination questions, annotated with SEG examiners' comments. (See note below.)

Useful Addresses

Sources of information for homework and coursework assignments are listed at the back of this *Resource File*.

NOTE ON SAMPLE EXAMINATION QUESTIONS

Whilst the student textbook includes Sample Examination Questions from several examination boards, all the example examination answers and examiners' comments included on the Study Skills Sheets of this *Teacher's Resource File* come from the SEG Short Course in Religious Education. SEG Grade Descriptions are explained on page 124 of this *Resource File*.

Introduction

The Activity Sheets on pages 10-15 are for use alongside the Introduction of *Thinking Through Religion*. The course aims to get students to think about religion and morality. Morality is all about informed choices between right and wrong. It does not exist in a vacuum. Each religion offers a worldview with its own value system. The worldview can be likened to the foundations of a house, or a map to guide a person through life. Thus, for religions, moral values are grounded in religious beliefs about the meaning of life, the nature of humanity, and, where appropriate, the nature of God.

Activity Sheet	Objective for students
Intro. 1 What do you believe?	To reflect on what they believe.
Intro. 2 Right and Wrong	To reflect on what they consider to be right and wrong.
Intro. 3 How do I decide?	To consider how they make choices about right and wrong. What influences them?
Intro. 4 Morality in the Media	To consider the power of the media in shaping ideas of right and wrong.

Preparing for your examination

Knowing what the examiners can ask

The syllabus for your examination (which your teacher will have) sets out the subjects on which you may be asked questions. But to see the *type of questions* that you will have to answer, look at copies of past examination papers. Make sure that you become familiar with the *structure of the paper*, *how many questions* you will have to answer, and *how long* you will be given to answer.

Deciding what to revise

From the syllabus and the old examination papers, you can tell what to revise. If the examination allows you to choose out of several questions on various subjects, you can decide which subjects you would most like to answer questions on and revise those subjects in particular detail.

Revising during the course

Revision should be something which you do throughout the course. It should not be left to the end when you have only two or three weeks to cram everything in. Revision for the final public examinations should be started three or four months before the examinations begin.

Throughout the course, when you finish studying each major topic, write your own summary revision notes. Some people find it helpful to use file cards. Others just list the main points learnt on a piece of file paper. Use subheadings and bullet points. If there is anything you do not understand, check it with your teacher straight away.

Design a revision programme taking advantage of school holidays. Divide what you have to learn into small manageable pieces.

Be sure to build short breaks and treats into this timetable. This will give you something to look forward to and will help concentrate your mind for the time you are revising. The treat can be anything from a piece of cake to a phonecall to a friend or listening to a CD.

Be realistic with your timetable. When you are memorising material, 40 minutes is a sensible amount of time in one stretch. After that, take a 10-minute break before starting again. Don't think that you can work for 10 hours a day!

Don't panic if you don't follow your timetable exactly. This is normal. But be aware of the progress you are making. Monitor your progress.

Stick to your revision times. Do not be tempted to give up revision periods for television or a long conversation on the phone.

The final countdown

Try to revise in a warm quiet place. Most people need silence when they revise, so do not try to revise whilst the television is on. Seek quietness. Libraries can be good places for concentrated periods of silence.

Try various techniques for memorising material:

- Learn key words which stimulate thoughts.
- Repeat the same material over and over again by reading, writing, and speaking aloud.
- Devise your own flow charts.
- Explain to a parent or friend what you are learning.
- Get someone to test you orally.

After you have revised a topic, try answering a test or a question from a past examination.

When you think you have learnt a topic, test yourself again after a 24-hour break. This will help to keep it in your memory.

Advice for your examination day

On the day of the examination:

- Eat a good breakfast. Brains need nourishment to work at their best.
- Dress comfortably. Do not wear too tight-fitting clothes, because exam rooms can be hot and stuffy.
- Make sure that you have all the materials for the exam. Check these before you leave your house. Take extra pens or pencils in case one runs out or breaks. Put all your materials in a clear plastic see-through bag.

When you receive the examination paper:

- Do not panic. Many exam papers look frightening when you first read them.
- Read the instructions carefully. Many pupils fail exams because they do not follow all the instructions. (Sometimes they answer too many questions, wasting valuable time.)
- Listen carefully to the instructions of the invigilator. Occasionally there is a printing error in the examination paper and the invigilator will tell you of corrections that need to be made.
- Spend the first five minutes reading through all the questions – and deciding which questions to answer.

Pacing yourself:

- If the exam is divided into parts, take care to spend the right amount of time on each part.
- Do not put all your efforts into answering the first few questions and leave insufficient time and energy for the remaining questions.
- You should answer all the questions you have to. It is better to attempt two essay questions incompletely than to answer one fully and the other not at all.

- During the exam, check the time now and then to make sure that you are on course to complete the paper.
- Try to finish writing 10 minutes before the end of the examination, so that you can spend this time reading through all your answers, correcting mistakes and adding details.

Before answering a question:

- Underline the key words and parts of the question.
- Read and re-read the question carefully and be sure that you have correctly understood what the examiner is asking. (For example, if the question asks you to give religious examples, you will not gain marks for just giving your opinion.)
- Remember that your exam is in RE. You must show that you know about the key religious beliefs and practices of the religion(s) you have studied, and how these can be applied to the issues you have studied.
- Take note of how many marks are being awarded for the question. This is an indication of how much detail you need to include.
- Remember not to waffle!
- Remember that, when a question asks for your opinion, you need to give reasons to support what you think. You should give a number of reasons and explain each in detail. You should also say something about the opposite point of view, and reasons which support it. To do well on these questions, you MUST develop your ideas sufficiently.

What do you believe?

Use the table to note down your thoughts in response to the
questions in the left-hand column.

	I believe . . .
Does God exist? If so, what is God like? Is there any evidence for the existence of God?	
Where did the world come from?	
Is there another world beside this one?	
Why was I born?	
Is there any meaning in life?	
How do people differ from animals?	
Are all people equal?	
What makes human life valuable?	

Is all human life valuable?	
When does human life begin?	
Why do people suffer? Is God responsible for all suffering in the world? Can anything good come from suffering?	
Is there a life after death? If so, what is it like?	
Do you think that people are or will be judged for what they have done in their life? If so, how does this judgement work?	
Do you think the world will come to an end? If so, what will the end of the world be like?	
Should people stand up for what they believe?	
Should religion affect politics?	

Right and Wrong

Use the table to note down what you think in response to the questions in the left-hand column. Think about and give your reasons, rather than just putting "yes" or "no" answers.

	I think . . .
Where do ideas about right and wrong come from?	
Should children obey their parents?	
Should you always forgive when you are wronged?	
Is it right to have sex outside marriage?	
What do you think about people having affairs?	
Is divorce ever right?	
Is abortion ever right?	
Is it the woman's choice if she has an abortion, or should other people be involved in the decision?	
Is it always wrong to take human life? Or are there circumstances in which it may be right to take human life? What do you think those circumstances are?	

What do you think about euthanasia (mercy killing)?	
Is war ever justified?	
Is there a difference between a soldier killing in battle and a murderer? If so, what is the difference?	
Is it OK to be gay?	
Does television harm young people?	
Do we have a responsibility to the world? If so, what?	
Should animals be used for testing medicines?	
Are all blood sports cruel?	
Is it right to eat meat? Why are some people vegetarian?	
Where are some people rich and others very poor? Do we have a responsibility towards the poor?	
Is it OK to play the National Lottery? Are there any dangers?	

How do I decide?

1 Think about the people and things that influence you when you make decisions about what is the right thing to do. Who or what has the strongest influence on you?

2 Which one of the statements here do you (a) most agree with, and (b) least agree with? Explain your choices.

3 Do you think any of the suggested ways of deciding what to do are unreliable? Explain why.

4 Choose a moral issue (e.g. abortion or going to war). What would the people who made the statements here think about the issue?

> I think about whether my action will hurt anyone else. If it will, I will not do it.

> What's important is the motive behind each action. Motives are as important as the actions themselves.

> It is important to be responsible in life.

> My conscience guides me.

> It's important to think about the rights of all people involved.

> I do what I see everybody else doing. If they're doing it, it mustn't be wrong.

> My religion is the most important guide.

> Most of the time I do what my feelings tell me to. It's a gut reaction.

> As you go through life you build up experience of what works and what doesn't. I make my decisions based on past experience.

> I get my ideas from television – soaps and things like that.

Morality in the Media

The media (newspapers, magazines, books, advertising, television, radio, and the internet) have a big influence in shaping people's ideas of right and wrong. They influence us in a number of ways: (a) by their choice of subjects to present to us; (b) by the way in which they present each subject; (c) by the images they use to illustrate each subject.

(Q)

1 Study the ways in which the media present a subject. (Choose a subject such as Family Life, Religion, Christianity, Famine, War . . .) Notice, for instance, what lifestyles and values are shown as "good" and "bad". Do you agree with the ideas presented? Make a chart, like the one below, to record your findings.

2 Do you think the media are being morally responsible in the messages they are conveying?

DID YOU KNOW?

On average, fathers spend 25 minutes each week and mothers spend 38 minutes each week in genuine conversation with their children. On average, children spend 21 hours each week watching television.

Messages in the Media about . . . .

Title of Newspaper, Magazine, Programme, Advertisement, etc	Date of publication or date seen	Description	Your opinion/evaluation

Understanding Christianity

St Paul tried to capture the essence of Christianity in his words to the Corinthians:

"I passed on to you what I received, which is of the greatest importance: that Christ died for our sins, as written in the Scriptures; that he was buried and that he was raised to life three days later, as written in the Scriptures; that he appeared to Peter and then to all twelve apostles."
[1 Corinthians 15: 3-5 GNB]

Here we have the unique message of Christianity in a nutshell: Jesus died for humanity's sins (in theological terms this is variously referred to as "the atonement" and "dying to save us – salvation"); Jesus rose again, showing God's power over evil and death; and he appeared to his disciples. Christians believe that God, in the form of the Holy Spirit, continues to be present with people.

Origins
The origins of Christianity lie in the life, ministry, death, resurrection, and ascension of Jesus. However, Christians trace their roots further back than this – to Judaism. Jesus was a Jewish teacher. His teaching is heavily rooted in Jewish scriptures. The Christian holy book, the Bible, incorporates the Jewish scriptures known as the Tenakh. Christians trace their origins to the covenants that God made with the Jewish people (hence the Old Testament/Covenant, and the New Testament/Covenant).

The Jewish-Christian chronology is often referred to as "Salvation History". It is the story of God calling people (a chosen people) to be His own. Through history, humanity has constantly turned away from God, rejecting His kingship in their lives. At first, God sent judges and then prophets to call His people back. When people did not respond, God sent His Son, Jesus, to save people from their sinful ways.

Christians believe that God descended to earth in the human form of Jesus. This doctrine is called the Incarnation. It was God's rescue mission. In fact, the name Jesus means "rescuer". Jesus came to call people back to God. However, in order that justice be done, Christians believe that a ransom had to be paid for all the sin that humanity commits. Jesus became this ransom on the cross. Through paying the cost of sin, Jesus made reconciliation with God possible. This is why Christians say that Jesus is their "Saviour".

Ethics
Christians believe that God's loving action in Jesus sets a standard and an example of how they should act. Christianity could be called "The Gospel of the Second Chance" since, in Jesus, God gave humanity a second chance to be at one with Him. Jesus preached a Gospel of the Second Chance. One of his most famous parables is that of the Prodigal Son, the dramatic story of how a loving father gave his wayward son a big second chance.

Activity Sheet	Key concept	Objective for students
1.1 The Birdcage	Redemption: the reason why Jesus came to earth	To learn about one way in which a Christian views the world, understanding that this is not the only way.
1.2 The Million Dollar Loan	God is a gracious God.	To learn about one way in which Christians picture God.
1.3 Napoleon and the Furrier	The Incarnation	To gain understanding of what it means for Christians to say that God became a human being in Jesus.
1.4 Forgiveness: a case study 1.5 Les Misérables	Truth and reconciliation in South Africa Forgiveness	To gain understanding of, and evaluate, the Christian concept of forgiveness.
1.6 Examination Practice	Love and forgiveness	To practise short-answer questions.
1.7 Thinking through Christianity	Revision task, key words	To revise key words and ideas in Christianity.

The Birdcage

A man was on the side of the road with a large birdcage. A boy noticed that the cage was full of birds of many kinds.

"Where did you get those birds?" he asked.

"Oh, all over the place," the man replied. "I lure them with crumbs and pretend I'm their friend. Then, when they are close, I net them and shove them into my cage."

"And what are you going to do with them now?" asked the boy.

The man grinned. "I'm going to prod them with sticks, and get them really mad so they fight and kill each other. Those that survive, I will kill. None will escape."

The boy looked steadily at the man. What made him do such things? He looked into the cruel, hard eyes. Then he looked at the birds, defenceless, without hope.

"Can I buy those birds?" the boy asked.

The man hid a smile, aware that he could be on to a good thing if he played his cards right.

"Well," he said hesitantly, "the cage is pretty expensive, and I spent a lot of time collecting these birds. I'll tell you what I'll do. I'll let you have the lot, birds, cage and all, for ten pounds and that jacket you're wearing."

The boy paused. Ten pounds was all he had, and the jacket was new and very special. In fact, it was his prized possession. Slowly, he took out the ten pounds and handed it over. Then, even more slowly, he took off his jacket, gave it one last look and handed that over too. And then (well, you've guessed it) he opened the door and let the birds go free.

The Enemy of the world, Satan, was on the side of life's road with a very large cage. The man coming towards him noticed that it was crammed full of people of every kind, young, old, from every race and nation.

"Where did you get these people?" the man asked.

"Oh, from all over the world," Satan replied. "I lure them with drink, drugs, lust, lies, anger, hate, love of money, and all manner of things. I pretend I'm their friend, out to give them a good time. Then, when I've hooked them, into the cage they go!"

"And what will you do with them now?" asked the man.

Satan grinned. "I'm going to prod them, provoke them, get them to hate and destroy each other. I'll stir up racial hatred, and defiance of law and order. I'll make people bored, lonely, dissatisfied, confused, and restless. It's easy. People will always listen to what I offer them and (what's better) blame God for the outcome!"

"And then what?" the man asked.

"Those who do not destroy themselves, I will destroy. None will escape me."

The man stepped forward. "Can I buy these people from you?" he asked.

Satan snarled: "Yes, but it will cost you your life."

So Jesus Christ, the Son of God, paid for your release, your freedom from Satan's trap, with His own life, on the cross at Calvary. The door is open, and anyone whom Satan has deceived and caged can be set free.

This story represents how some Christians view the world, and how some Christians explain the death of Jesus on the cross.

1 Do you agree with the idea in the story that we are affected by a power outside ourselves to do wrong things?

2 Do you believe in the Devil? Explain your answer.

3 What does this story teach about why Jesus died on the cross?

4 Do you think the story provides a good explanation for the way the world is? Give reasons to support your answer.

The Million Dollar Loan

At the turn of the 1990s an entrepreneur in Los Angeles, USA, decided to cash in on people's desire for adventure travel. He had the idea of designing trips to the Seven Wonders of the Ancient World. There are no traces of most of these ancient wonders, but in Iraq there are moves to restore the Hanging Gardens of Babylon.

The entrepreneur organised a charter plane, accommodation, and professional guides. He invested in expensive television advertising. In order to finance his dream, he arranged a one million dollar loan from a venture capitalist. He calculated that, after the fourth trip to the Hanging Gardens, he would have covered operating costs and could start to pay back the loan.

There was only one thing which he left out of his calculations. Two weeks before the first trip, the Iraqi dictator Saddam Hussein invaded the neighbouring country of Kuwait, and the United States State Department banned all trips to Iraq.

The entrepreneur's dream had come to a sudden end. But he had invested all the capital he had borrowed. He did not know how he was going to pay back his million dollar loan. Finally, he put together a plan which would commit him to paying back $5,000 a month for the rest of his life. However, as he drew up an agreement about this, he realised that it still wouldn't be enough to pay back the loan. Anyway, where would he get the monthly payments from?

He decided there was no way around it. He went to his financial backer and confessed that his plan had gone terribly wrong. He started to discuss his repayment plans, his palms breaking out in a sweat as he realised the foolishness of what he was saying. The venture capitalist held up a hand to stop him: "Wait. What nonsense are you talking about? Repayment? Don't be silly. I'm a speculator. I win some. I lose some. I knew your plan had risks. It was a good idea though, and it is hardly your fault that a war has broken out. Just forget it."

Christians describe God as "gracious" or "showing grace". The story of the Million Dollar Loan is an illustration of grace in action.

1 What is your reaction to the story? How did the venture capitalist show grace? Do you think he or she was right to do so? What would you have done if you were (a) the entrepreneur, and (b) the venture capitalist?

2 Write a definition of the word grace. In what ways do you think God shows grace?

Napoleon and the Furrier

During Napoleon's invasion of Russia (1812), his troops were battling in the middle of yet another small town in that endless wintry land, when he was accidentally separated from his men. A group of Russian Cossacks spotted him and began chasing him through the twisting streets.

Napoleon ran for his life and ducked into a little furrier's shop in a side alley. As Napoleon entered the shop, gasping for breath, he saw the furrier and cried, "Save me! Save me! Where can I hide?" The furrier said, "Quick, under this big pile of furs in the corner!" and he covered Napoleon with many furs.

No sooner had he finished than the Russian Cossacks burst in, shouting "Where is he? We saw him come in." Despite the furrier's protests, they tore his shop apart, trying to find Napoleon. They poked into the pile of furs with their swords but didn't find him. Soon, they gave up and left.

After some time, Napoleon crept out from under the furs, unharmed, just as his personal guards came through the door. The furrier turned to Napoleon and said timidly, "Excuse me for asking this question of such a great man, but what was it like to be under those furs, knowing that the next moment would surely be your last?"

Napoleon drew himself up to his full height and said to the furrier indignantly, "How could you ask such a question of me, the Emperor Napoleon! Guards, take this impudent man out, blindfold him, and execute him. I, myself, will personally give the command to fire!"

The guards grabbed the poor furrier, dragged him outside, stood him up against a wall, and blindfolded him. The furrier could see nothing, but he could hear the movements of the guards as they shuffled into a line and prepared their rifles. He could hear the soft ruffling sound of his own clothing in the cold wind, he could feel the wind tugging gently at his clothes and chilling his face, and he was aware of an uncontrollable trembling in his legs. Then he heard Napoleon clear his throat and call out slowly, "Ready . . . aim . . .". In that moment, knowing that even those few sensations were about to be taken from him forever, a feeling that he couldn't describe welled up, as tears poured down his cheeks.

After a long silence, the furrier heard footsteps approaching him and the blindfold was stripped from his eyes. The sudden sunlight partially blinded him, but he saw Napoleon's eyes look intently into his own – seeming to see into every dusty corner of his being. Then Napoleon said softly, "Now you know."

1 In this true story, what lesson did Napoleon teach the furrier?

2 Christians believe that God became a human being and lived on earth in the person of Jesus, His son. Can you explain how the story of Napoleon and the Furrier helps to illustrate the importance for Christians of the belief that God was born in human form and died on a cross?

Forgiveness: a case study – South Africa

At the heart of the Christian ethic is Jesus's command to forgive your enemies and pray for those who persecute you. But what does this mean in practice? On this sheet you will learn how the people of South Africa have worked with the concept of forgiveness to create a new society after the apartheid era.

Apartheid

From 1948, the white government of South Africa set up the system of apartheid. The word "apartheid" means "separateness" in the Afrikaans language and describes the dividing of the South African people along racial lines, with different rights for different races. The black (African, Coloured, and Indian) population was discriminated against in many ways. Blacks were uprooted from their communities and placed in black townships. Black people were denied jobs, adequate housing, health care, and schooling. The apartheid system stripped blacks of their human dignity. Black people were subject to acts of violence. For instance, there were cases of tyre "necklaces" being tied around their necks, filled with petrol, and set alight.

The apartheid system officially came to an end in November 1993. The elections of April 1994, when people of all races were allowed to vote, were South Africa's turning-point. They marked the beginning of a new democratic, non-racial, non-sexist South Africa. The issue that remained to be addressed was how to deal with the apartheid legacy. How was South Africa to deal with its violent and racially torn past? There were several options.

Option 1: Bringing criminals to justice

Some people in South Africa wanted to follow the example of what happened to Nazi criminals after the Second World War: they were tried for acts against humanity in the Nuremberg Trials (1945). This option was rejected because it would lead to resentment among the white population. The new South Africa was to be a society where white and black people live together in harmony.

Option 2: Letting bygones be bygones

One way of starting anew is to let the past remain in the past. Many whites who had been in the security forces during apartheid favoured this option. However, it was rejected because it would victimise the victims of apartheid a second time round. It would mean denying their horrific experiences.

Option 3: Conditional amnesty

The third option – which was accepted – was to grant an amnesty (a pardon) to all individuals who took part in criminal acts under the apartheid regime, in exchange for their coming forward and speaking the truth about what they had done. In this way criminals were offered freedom in exchange for telling the truth. If people did not come forward, they would face the risk of being caught and given long prison sentences.

The Truth and Reconciliation Commission

On 15 December 1995, the new South African President, Nelson Mandela, established the Truth and Reconciliation Commission, under the chairmanship of Archbishop Desmond Tutu. Its aim was to help South Africans come to terms with the past and to advance the cause of reconciliation, and a restoration of broken relationships between black and white South Africans. A series of hearings which continued until April 1998 received 15,000 statements from victims of apartheid and 7,000 applications for amnesty.

1 What was apartheid? How did it affect South Africa? You may like to look at an encyclopedia or the Internet to find out more.

2 Read through the three options that South Africa faced. Which would you have chosen? Give your reasons.

3 What do you think of the third option? What are the advantages and disadvantages of this option?

4 Do you think the approach of the Truth and Reconciliation Commission encourages people to think that it was all right to commit crimes because they would get a pardon? Is it ever right for criminals to merely apologise and be humiliated through public exposure?

5 Do you think the Truth and Reconciliation Commission achieved justice?

6 Do you think it is right for a country to forgive on behalf of all the victims who suffered?

Les Misérables

Narrator: *Les Misérables* is one of the most popular musicals today. Based on a 19th-century novel by Victor Hugo, it tells the story of Jean Valjean, a French prisoner, who is transformed by the power of being forgiven.

In the story, Valjean is sentenced when he is 19 years old for the crime of stealing bread. In prison he becomes a hardened man, feared by the other inmates. At last he earns his release. Convicts in those days had to carry identity cards and no innkeeper would let a dangerous prisoner spend the night under his roof. So Valjean wanders the village roads, seeking shelter against the weather, until, after four days, a kindly bishop has mercy on him.

That night Valjean lies still until the bishop and his sister have drifted off to sleep. Then he rises from his bed, steals the family silver, and creeps off into the darkness.

The next morning three policemen knock on the bishop's door, with Valjean in tow. They have caught the convict with the silver and are ready to put him in chains for life. However, the bishop responds in a way that no one, especially Valjean, expects:

Bishop: So here you are! I'm delighted to see you. Had you forgotten that I gave you the candlesticks as well? They're silver like the rest, and worth a good 200 francs. Did you forget to take them?

Narrator: Valjean stares at the bishop, unable to believe what he has heard.

Bishop: Valjean is no thief. This silver was my gift to him.

Narrator: When the police withdraw, the bishop gives the candlesticks to his guest, who is now speechless and trembling.

Bishop: Do not forget – do not ever forget – that you have promised me to use the money you make from what I have given you to make yourself an honest man.

Narrator: The power of the bishop's act changes Valjean's life forever. He feels forgiven, even though he has never asked for forgiveness. He keeps the candlesticks as a precious memory and dedicates himself from then on to helping others in need.

However, this is not the end of the story. In the original novel a detective named Javert is angered by the forgiveness which the bishop shows Valjean. Over the next two decades Javert stalks Valjean. Javert is consumed by a thirst for retribution. When Valjean saves Javert's life, the detective senses that his black-and-white world is beginning to crumble. Unable to cope with such an act, Javert jumps off a bridge into the River Seine.

1 Why do you think Valjean became hardened in prison? What made Valjean steal from the bishop who was helping him?

2 What qualities must the bishop have had to forgive Valjean? Do you think the bishop was right to grant forgiveness without Valjean saying sorry? What does this tell you about the nature of Christian forgiveness?

3 In what ways did Valjean change as a result of his encounter with the bishop? How was the bishop different from the detective Javert?

Examination Practice:
Christian Ethics: attitudes to Love and Forgiveness

Questions (a) – (d) can be answered in a single word, phrase, or sentence. Question (e) requires a longer answer.

(a) Who wrote the words "Love is patient and kind"? [1 mark]

(b) In Mark Chapter 12, what does Jesus say is the second commandment? [1 mark]

(c) In Luke Chapter 23, what reason does Jesus give for forgiving his executioners? [1 mark]

(d) What does the Lord's Prayer teach Christians about forgiveness? [2 marks]

(e) "When you think about it, forgiveness benefits the forgiver more than the forgiven."
How far do you agree with this statement? Show that you have thought about different points of view, giving reasons to support your answer. [5 marks]

[SEG, Summer 1997]

Thinking through Christianity

Revision Task

In groups choose one of the boxes. Prepare and present a short talk explaining the words in your box. Use your notes and information in the *Thinking Through Religion* textbook to help you. You might also present pictures to illustrate the meanings of the words.

CONCEPTS

Salvation: being saved by God from evil and everlasting death

Heaven: the place, or state, in which souls will be united with God

Hell: the place, or state, in which souls will be separated from God

Eternal Life: the state into which Christians believe they will pass after they die

Church: the whole community of Christians; or a building in which Christians worship

Easter: central Christian festival which celebrates the resurrection of Jesus

Holy Communion: central liturgical service observed by most churches. It is also referred to as Eucharist, Mass, Lord's Supper, Divine Liturgy. It recalls the last meal of Jesus and celebrates his sacrificial death.

HOLY BOOKS

Bible: made up of the Old Testament and the New Testament

Old Testament: collection of 39 books shared with Judaism

New Testament: collection of 27 books containing accounts of the life and death of Christ and the history of the early Church

KEY BELIEFS

God as Creator and Sustainer: belief that God created the world out of nothing and that God still actively cares about the world

Trinity: doctrine of the three-fold nature of God – Father, Son, and Holy Spirit

Incarnation: the doctrine that God took human form in Jesus

Christ: "the anointed (chosen) one"– a title applied to Jesus by his followers

Holy Spirit: third person of the Trinity; God's divine presence and power in the world

Resurrection: the rising from the dead of Jesus on the third day after his crucifixion. The word resurrection also refers to the rising from the dead of believers at the Last Day.

MORALITY

Agape: selfless love towards others – loving people because God loves them

Forgiveness: a love that puts hurt and revenge aside and heals broken relationships

Justice: Christians believe that God is a just God. They therefore believe that Christians should speak out against all forms of injustice. God is on the side of all who are oppressed. Christians believe that God will right the world's wrongs at the end of time.

Image of God: Christians believe that each person is made in God's image and that, therefore, all people are precious and of equal worth.

Stewardship: Christians believe that the world is God's and that God loves the world. People are to be responsible stewards of the world and its resources.

Understanding Buddhism

"What is the essence of Buddhism? Quite simply, it is the great question of who or what we are, right here, now, at this very moment. For you, the reader, this means nothing other than who or what is right now looking at these printed words on the page of this book. Reflect on that for a moment . . . who is the reader that is looking at them?"

[John Snelling, *The Buddhist Handbook*, Century Paperbacks, 1987]

Who am I? What am I? Why am I here? Where am I going? Teenagers often ask these questions. The forming of our individual identity, the coming to understand who exactly we are, is part of our quest in teenage. And the quest does not end when we finish school. These are spiritual questions that stay with us throughout life.

Let us return to John Snelling's words and try to answer his question. Many people will have no doubt who is reading these words. They call that person "I" or "me". They have a name, a personal biography, a job, a nationality, and a family. This is who they are. But reflect further. Concentrate on being the reader of these words, here and now. Your name, nationality, job, or family are not at the front of your mind. These things are not actually important to you in the here and now, just concentrating on these words. Right now, are you any more than a collection of transitory thoughts and memories trying to concentrate on these words?

These thoughts might be starting to make you feel uneasy. You may even feel a little excited at seeing the mystery of who we are in a new way. This goes to the heart of Buddhism – the search to unravel who we really are. As we begin to explore who we really are, we come to question what is really there in the world at all. Buddhism is about becoming aware of what really is. Meditation is the process through which people become aware. The result is enlightenment. The historical Buddha, Siddattha Gautama, is called the Buddha because he is the "awakened", or "enlightened", one.

Origins

Buddhism is a child of the spirituality of India. It began in the 6th century BCE, with the enlightenment of Siddattha Gautama. He was persuaded to share the truth of, and the way to, enlightenment. His teaching (dhamma) became the foundation for Buddhism. "Buddhism" is actually a Western term. It is better called "Buddha-dhamma" or "Buddha-sasana". The Buddha saw himself as a physician and a guide. He diagnosed what was wrong with the world and pointed towards the way of recovery – enlightenment.

Ethics

The Buddha was born into Hinduism. Buddhism arises out of Hinduism and shares many characteristics with it. For example, both religions believe in many cycles of time, and in long periods through which a person is reborn. A number of concepts are shared by Hinduism and Buddhism: samsara (the cycle of birth, death, and rebirth), karma (action and its consequences), moksha (liberation). However, the Buddha modified many Hindu concepts. He saw all things as characterised by dukkha (unsatisfactoriness) and anicca (impermanence). It follows that there is no such thing as a soul which remains permanent – even we ourselves are transitory. It follows also that there cannot be an eternal God.

Many people have debated whether Buddhism can be regarded as a religion, when it does not believe in a Supreme Being who created the world and the creatures within it, nor in a personal soul. Such a definition of religion may be too narrow. Buddhism as a lived experience is crucial. Buddhism regards the religious life as essentially a course in self-transformation. It emphasises meditation. Furthermore, Buddhism is widely respected as one of the most ethical religions. At the core of Buddhist ethics is ahimsa (non-harming). This has far-reaching results. It leads Buddhists into founding hospitals, protesting against any form of violence and war, and in many cases into being vegetarian.

Activity Sheet	Key concept	Objective for students
2. 1 Three Precious Jewels	Buddha, Dhamma, Sangha	To learn about three central concepts.
2. 2 Living in the Present	Being aware/enlightened	To learn about Right Awareness and to reflect on how this concept can help each one of us.
2. 3 Five Journeys	Buddhist way of life/ethics	To reflect on life from a Buddhist perspective.
2. 4 Thinking through Buddhism	Revision task	To revise key words and concepts in Buddhism.

Three Precious Jewels

Buddha, Dhamma, and Sangha (known as the three Precious Jewels or the three Refuges) are the central concepts in Buddhism.

1. The Buddha

The man: Siddattha Gautama was born in a village called Lumbini in northern India, in about 563 BCE. Buddhists believe Siddattha to be the 24th Buddha in the present stage of the world. When his teachings are no longer popular, another Buddha, called Maitreya, will come.

Early Life: Siddattha Gautama was born into a royal family. His father, Suddhodana, was the leader of a local people known as the Shakyas. Not long after Siddattha's birth, a wise man named Asita visited the family and proclaimed that the boy would grow up to be an enlightened being. His father was not happy, since he knew that it would be the painful things in life which would make his son religious. He therefore brought up Siddattha in the greatest luxury, with no pain in sight.

Four Sights: Siddattha married his beautiful young cousin, Yasodhara and, when he was about 29, they had a son whom they named Rahula. The choice of this name (which means "chains") was an indication that Siddattha was restless with all his luxury. He arranged to make four trips into the outside world, which until now he had never seen. On these trips he saw (a) an old man, (b) a sick man, and (c) a dead man. The effect of these sights was life-changing. For the first time Siddattha realised that life was made up of suffering, and that he himself would become sick, grow old, and die one day.

On the fourth trip he saw a sadhu, a wandering holy man, such as can be seen throughout India today. This holy man possessed nothing materially, but he had an inner happiness which greatly impressed Siddattha. Old age, sickness, and death did not frighten the sadhu. Siddattha knew that he had to go in search of this inner happiness. At the age of 29, he left his rich life-style and became a wandering, homeless pilgrim. He learned all that he could from religious teachers, but this did not give him the answers he needed. He joined a group of ascetics – men who tried to control their body by mental and physical discipline and thus overcome suffering. All this resulted in his nearly killing himself through starvation.

The Middle Way: Siddattha realised that there must be a middle way between the extremes of having everything and having nothing. At a place which today is called Bodh Gaya, Siddattha decided to sit in meditation until he found an answer. As he meditated he became enlightened about the Truth of suffering and the way to end suffering. He was 35 years old. For the next 45 years he taught others to become enlightened. His teaching is known as the Dhamma.

2. The Dhamma

At the heart of the Buddha's teaching, the Dhamma, are the Four Noble Truths and the Eightfold Path. (See pages 36-37 of the *Thinking Through Religion* textbook.)

3. The Sangha

A common symbol for the Dhamma is the lotus. The lotus symbol is used in pictures, above the Buddha. From the lotus flower in such pictures, there rises a small figure of a monk, who represents the Sangha.

The Buddhist Sangha today is made up of monks (called bhikkhus) and nuns (called bhikkhunis). Some Sanghas also include lay people.

The Buddha taught: "Go forth, O monks, to bless the many, to bring happiness to the many, out of compassion for the worlds; go forth for the welfare, the blessing, the happiness of all beings . . . Go forth and spread the teaching that is beautiful."

1 Is Siddattha Gautama the only Buddha who has existed? Why did his father bring him up in the greatest luxury? In what way did the four sights influence Siddattha? Why did Siddattha leave his palace when he was 29? Why did he join the ascetics? Why did their way not satisfy him?

2 Why is Buddhism called the Middle Way?

3 In the quotation from the Buddha to his monks, what type of happiness is the Buddha talking about? Why do you think the Buddha's teaching is called beautiful? What does the quotation say about what his teaching tries to achieve?

Living in the Present

The most important turning-point in the Buddha's life was when he meditated under the Bodhi tree and became "enlightened". This word means that he saw the way things really are. He reached an understanding about what really matters in life. From this position of understanding he started to teach others what he had learnt. His main teaching is summed up in the **Four Noble Truths**. The fourth Noble Truth states that the way to end suffering, and find inner happiness, is to follow the **Eightfold Path**.

One of the eight elements of the path is **Right Awareness** – being awake to the present moment and living it as it is; being aware of how things are and of what you are thinking, feeling, and doing now, so that you do not later regret how you behave.

The following reading about time explores what it might mean to live in the present.

> Yesterday is history
> Tomorrow a mystery
> Today is a gift
> That's why it's called the present!

> The clock is running. Make the most of today.

TIME

To realise the value of ONE YEAR,
  ask a senior student who missed a college application deadline.

To realise the value of ONE MONTH,
  ask a mother who has given birth to a premature baby.

To realise the value of ONE WEEK,
  ask an editor of a weekly newspaper.

To realise the value of ONE DAY,
  ask the daily wage labourer who has kids to feed.

To realise the value of ONE HOUR,
  ask the lovers who are waiting to meet.

To realise the value of ONE MINUTE,
  ask a person who has missed the train.

To realise the value of ONE SECOND,
  ask a person who has avoided an accident.

To realise the value of ONE MILLI-SECOND,
  ask the person who has won a silver medal in the Olympics.

Treasure every moment that you have!

1 What does it mean to be aware?

2 Write your own poem or story which captures what it means to live in the present.

3 If you knew you were only going to live for a short amount of time, would you do anything different in your life today? Would you change the effort you put into your relationships?

Five Journeys

An urgent call came to the great Lama (spiritual leader) of the North, asking for a wise and holy teacher to be sent to instruct young people in the South about the purpose of living. To everyone's astonishment, the Lama sent five teachers instead of one. He explained mysteriously: "We shall be fortunate if one of them gets to the South."

The group of five set off. After several days a messenger came running up to them and cried: "There is a terrible famine in our village. The rains and the crops have failed. Both beasts and people are starving. Many have already died. Stay with us, we beg you. Care for us. Teach us knowledge of science and of nature."

"I would not be a Buddhist," said one of the five teachers sent by the Lama of the North, "if I did not stop here, and provide knowledge and assistance for these suffering people." The other four continued.

A few days later the four came to a city where some of the people on the streets pleaded with them: "The governors of this city are uncaring and cruel. Stay with us here, we beg you, and help us to resist and to replace the people in power here, and to govern ourselves in justice and in peace."

"I would not be a Buddhist," said one of the teachers sent by the Lama of the North, "if I did not stop here, and join in resistance, politics, and government." The other three continued.

Some days later the three came to a town where there were frantic quarrels and arguments amongst members of different religious groups. "Help us, we beg you," said some of the people, "to understand and to tolerate each other's festivals and customs so that each person here feels rooted in their own tradition and history, but also feels respect for the traditions and stories of others."

"I would not be a Buddhist," said one of the teachers sent by the Lama of the North, "if I did not stop here, and help the people to calm down, and to live with each other in harmony and peace." The other two continued.

A few days later the two came to a small settlement where all the people seemed marvellously happy. There were dances and games, paintings and music, embraces and laughter. Everyone had challenging and valuable work. "Settle with us here, we beg you," said the people. "Set up home here. Enjoy sexual love. Nurture and cherish new human beings. Join us here in building the future."

"I would not be a Buddhist," said one of the teachers sent by the Lama of the North, "if I did not stop and make my dwelling here, and enjoy the pleasures of everyday life." The other continued.

Eventually the fifth teacher reached the Lama of the South, and began there the work which had been requested, and which was required – that of instructing the young people about the purpose of living.

1 (a) What do you think the purpose of life is?
   (b) What purposes of life are suggested in this story?

2 Why did four of the teachers not reach the South? What do you think of the reasons they gave? Were they justified?

3 What might the fifth teacher say about the other four teachers when he reached the South? Was his journey more important than the journeys of the other four?

Thinking through Buddhism

Revision Task

In groups choose one of the boxes. Prepare and present a short talk explaining the words or statements in your box. Use your notes and information in the *Thinking Through Religion* textbook to help you. You might also present pictures to illustrate the meanings of the words.

CONCEPTS

The Three Jewels/Refuges

1. **Buddha:** enlightened/awakened one

2. **Dhamma:** teachings, the way things are

3. **Sangha:** the Buddhist community, of monks, nuns, and lay people

Karma: actions (what you sow you shall reap)

Samsara: cycle of birth, death, rebirth

Nibbana: state of peace

Metta: loving-kindness

HOLY BOOKS

Sutta: "thread", "topic", or "single idea"; refers to Buddhist religious texts

Pali Canon/ Tipitaka: the three "baskets" containing the holy books:

1. **Vinaya Pitaka** – Discipline, rules of life
2. **Sutta Pitaka** – containing the teachings of the Buddha
3. **Abhidhamma Pitaka** – containing discussions on how to understand and interpret the Buddha's teachings

KEY BELIEFS

The Three Marks of Existence

1. **Anicca:** Everything changes and nothing lasts forever.

2. **Dukkha:** Life is unsatisfactory.

3. **Anatta** There is no such thing as the self.

The Four Noble Truths: Dukkha is part of everyday life. Dukkha is caused by wanting. Dukkha can be ended. It can be ended by following the Eightfold Path.

The Eightfold Path:
1) Right Understanding
2) Right Attitude
3) Right Speech
4) Right Action
5) Right Livelihood
6) Right Effort
7) Right Awareness
8) Right Concentration

MORALITY

Right Action, summed up in the **Five Precepts** by which all Buddhists try to live:
1. I will not harm living beings.
2. I will not take what is not given.
3. I will avoid harmful sexual activity.
4. I will avoid using words in incorrect ways.
5. I will not take drugs or drink that confuse the mind.

Understanding Hinduism

Origins

Hinduism has its roots in India. The words India and Hindu are closely linked with the name of the River Indus. Hindu was the name given by outsiders to the way of life of the people of India. Hindus themselves prefer to call their way of life **Sanatana Dharma** – which means "eternal law". The earliest origins of Hinduism are said to be in the ancient civilisation of the Indus Valley, which thrived over 4,000 years ago. This civilisation was built on the prosperity of an agriculturally rich community. We do not know much about the religion of the people. However, archaeologists have uncovered clay figures which appear to represent a mother goddess or a goddess of fertility. There is also evidence of large bathing pools, which may have had a ritual function. Reverence for God as Mother and the practice of ritual washing are important in Hindu belief and life today.

Another way of life and another group of people helped to shape the early beginnings of Hinduism from about 1500 BCE. These people were nomads, travellers, and warriors on horseback, known as the Aryans. Some say the Aryans invaded India, coming down from the north. The Aryans worshipped the divine in the powers of nature. They prayed to Agni, the god of fire, and Indra, the god of the storm. Their hymns to the gods remain as part of the most sacred Hindu scriptures.

Scriptures

There is no single founder or prophet in Hinduism and there is no single holy book. There are several sacred scriptures and these divide into two groups. One group of texts is called **shruti** which means "revealed". Hindus believe that the words of these texts were revealed to the holy men of ancient India. The shruti scriptures contain the **Vedas**. These hymns to the gods are the most ancient and most sacred of Hindu scriptures. The shruti texts also include the **Upanishads**. These are discussions on the mysteries of life, the universe, and God. The word Upanishad means to "sit down near". The Upanishads were passed down from the holy men to those who came to sit and listen in their search for the way to the truth.

The other strand of scriptures is called **smriti**, which means "remembered". Smriti texts include the story of the **Mahabharata**. The best-loved of all Hindu scriptures is the **Bhagavad Gita**, the song of Lord Krishna, which is contained within the Mahabharata. Many Hindus believe that Krishna was God in human form. The **Ramayana** is another well-known story from the smriti texts. It tells of Prince Rama's victory over evil and sets him as a perfect role model for Hindus to follow. The **Laws of Manu** are usually regarded as smriti scripture. These texts offer guidance on how to live and what to do at each age and stage in life.

The Supreme Spirit

Given the long history of the tradition and the vastness of the Indian sub-continent, it is not surprising that there is great diversity of practice and belief within Hinduism. Most Hindus believe in the one Supreme Spirit, Brahman. This Spirit is present in all life as individual soul or Atman. The soul, like Brahman, is eternal and survives death to be born again in another body.

Activity Sheet		Key concept	Objective for students
3.1	The T-Shirt Tiff: Gaudy or Godly?	Respect for deities	To think about religious respect by considering a case of differing sensibilities.
3.2	Non-violence	Ahimsa	To consider the meaning of non-violence in thought, word, and deed; and how the principle can be applied in today's world.
3.3	Thinking through Hinduism	Revision task	To revise key words and concepts in Hinduism.

The T-Shirt Tiff: Gaudy or Godly?

Concern over fashion fad

SHIRTS and skirts with lavish images of Hindu deities sold in Malaysia should be banned, say outraged members of the Malaysia Hindu Sangam.

Some Hindus entering tourist shops on Penang Road in Penang, Malaysia, were shocked to find T-shirts, "disco blouses" and mini-skirts decorated with images of Hindu gods and goddesses. Calling the clothes "degrading and insulting to the Hindu religion", the Malaysia Hindu Sangam launched a campaign to prohibit the fashion fad.

The clothes, imported from Hong Kong and Thailand, display traditional and highly artistic images of Ganesh, Durga, Vishnu, Krishna, and Shiva. The stylish T-shirts come in a rainbow of colours and styles. Many are printed solid, front and back, making a strong visual impact, and cost about US $5 each.

The sale of these garments is felt to be not only offensive to Hindus but also a cheap and degrading sales gimmick. It is using religion for commercial gain. Murugiah, chairman of the Sensitive Issues Committee of the Malaysia Hindu Sangam, went on to state that the clothes are especially popular with tourists, who are the main buyers.

Other parts of the world have different views. In the island of Mauritius, just off the coast of Madagascar, devotees frequently go to the temple wearing "deity T-shirts". To them, it is acceptable devotional Hindu dress. A Sri Lankan family from Saskathewan, Canada, visited the *Hinduism Today* offices in Hawaii recently wearing a Ganesh and Lakshmi T-shirt bought in Virginia. The mother confessed that she has worn the shirts to work, where her colleagues asked respectful questions.

Hindus like Vasanthy Perakasam of Kuala Lumpur worry that it "could be a strategy to demean our gods and make others laugh at them". Her husband, Selladurai Perakasam, agreed but admitted: "It could also be an opportunity for adults or children to get to know our many gods and provide a chance for a non-Hindu to ask about the deity. We need to have a very open mind about our religion and defend it when necessary but not over-protect it."

As a result of complaints, Domestic Trade and Consumer Affairs Minister Datuk S. Subramaniam ordered the Trade Enforcement Division to take action and confiscate the mini-skirts and "disco blouses". T-shirts, however, are still being sold.

[Copyright *Hinduism Today International*, July 1999, used with permission]

1 Why are some Hindus asking for some designs on T-shirts and disco blouses to be banned? What do you think some Hindus meant when they said that the clothes were "degrading and insulting to the Hindu religion"? How can clothes insult?

2 Hindus believe that people can find the presence of God everywhere and that God pervades everything. In what ways do you think this belief should affect reactions to the "deity T-shirts"?

3 Do you think religious believers should dress in a certain way when they worship God? Explain your answer.

Non-violence

One of the greatest moral principles which Hinduism has to offer the world today is that of ahimsa. Ahimsa is the Sanskrit word for non-violence – that is, non-violence in thought, word, and deed. It is an ideal: something for people to aim for, just as A+ in all subjects at school is an ideal that students might try to achieve. Ideals might not always be possible to achieve, but they are worth aiming for.

Probably the greatest Hindu proponent of ahimsa in the 20th century was the Indian leader Mahatma Gandhi (1869-1948). His emphasis on ahimsa had a great effect on other world leaders, including Martin Luther King and Nelson Mandela.

The Gandhi Institute for Non-violence was formed by Arun Gandhi, the grandson of Mahatma Gandhi, to promote and apply the principles of non-violence locally, nationally, and globally. Below are some extracts from an interview with Arun Gandhi held in 1998.

India's Defiance: at what price?

Last week India shocked the world by exploding five nuclear devices underneath the Rajasthan desert. That led Pakistan to announce plans for testing a nuclear device this week, and it set off a storm of international protests, threats and sanctions against India. Thus the nation whose "father", Mahatma Gandhi, is an international symbol for non-violence, has shown it belongs to the world's most exclusive club: the nuclear powers.

THE PATH OF THE SATYAGRAHA

Mahatma Gandhi encouraged his followers to adopt the path of the satyagraha, one who overcomes evil without violence:

"A satyagraha must never forget the distinction between evil and the evil doer. He must not harbour ill-will or bitterness against the latter. He may not even employ needlessly offensive language against the evil person . . . a satyagraha will always try to overcome evil by good, anger by love, untruth by truth, Himsa by Ahimsa."
[Gandhi, *The Science of Satyagraha*]

1 What do you think it means to have non-violence in thought, word, and deed?

AN INTERVIEW WITH ARUN GANDHI

How would Mahatma Gandhi have felt about India exploding nuclear devices?

Arun: He would be very distressed. He wanted the government to adopt non-violence as a way of life and show the world that non-violence can be applied in all circumstances. He didn't want partition [of India and Pakistan, in 1949]; he was willing to wait and gain independence for a united country. He felt that Hindus and Muslims could live together in peace. He didn't want all this Western materialism to creep into India. He felt we could live simpler and more moral and meaningful lives. India totally rejected all of that.

I don't think that we need to look at it just from this one perspective of India behaving immorally. The whole problem is that we have created this kind of psychosis. The United States and the Soviet Union during the Cold War period created this Frankenstein monster, and now they are not able to control it. This is what grandfather had said: violence only leads to more violence. We won't be able to control it until we destroy ourselves. Creating weapons of destruction will destroy our souls, our humanity, and us physically even. That is true for everybody.

Continued

The alternative is for the people to wake up and realise that all of these things that the politicians use to control and exploit us, that we don't need any of this, that we're going to take our destiny in our own hands.

Indian officials say nuclear capability is necessary to deter aggression from neighbouring China and Pakistan. Aren't those threats real?

Arun: I don't think these days anybody is interested in capturing another country. That myth of history has passed. If we create good neighbourliness and good relations with other people, we can live in harmony. We create these myths, we create these enmities, and we become pawns in the hands of both politicians and business people. We play into their hands by following them like sheep. Violence has become a big industry. Gun manufacturing and all these other things have to survive somehow, so they have to create these myths and keep people fighting, so they can produce weapons and sell them. All this is myth, that we can't live together peacefully.

Everything that we do now is based on the profit motive. People don't matter, people are dispensable, profit is not. We see it even in this country. When big corporations start downsizing, their only motive is to increase their profit. We manufacture all kinds of things that are useless and worthless; we don't see the moral aspect of it at all.

Some people will say your views are naive. The idea of non-violence is nice, but it is unrealistic in the face of threats to national security.

Arun: When Edison invented electric light bulbs, there were people who said it was all naive and stupid, that a bulb could never make light. The same thing with telephones. These things were once considered impossible, but today they have become part of our lives, and we don't even think of how we have come to this point. It's human nature to dismiss everything we don't understand as naive and impractical. But then it becomes practical. It becomes a way of life, and nobody thinks about it. Ultimately, it's the responsibility of every individual to decide if they want to change or if they want to flow with the tide.

[First published in the *San Jose Mercury News*, 17 May 1998]

Q

2 What do you think Arun Gandhi meant when he described a "Frankenstein monster"?

3 In what ways does he suggest that big businesses (corporations) are failing to apply the principle of ahimsa?

4 Do you think it is practical to apply the principle of ahimsa, locally, nationally, and globally, today?

Thinking through Hinduism

Revision Task

In groups choose one of the boxes. Prepare and present a short talk explaining the words in your box. Use your notes and information in the *Thinking Through Religion* textbook to help you. You might also present pictures to illustrate the meanings of the words.

CONCEPTS

Sanatana Dharma:	Hinduism is often called this – it means the eternal law; it refers to the universal and revealed nature of religion.
Guru:	spiritual teacher
Yoga:	union of the soul with God
Bhakti:	devotion, love; devotional form of Hinduism
Mantra:	a short sacred text or prayer which is continuously repeated
Puja:	worship

HOLY BOOKS

Vedas:	philosophical writings, the most ancient and most sacred of the Hindu scriptures
Upanishads:	sacred texts based on the teaching of a guru to a disciple. The Upanishads explain the teachings of the Vedas.
Mahabharata:	epic telling of the war between the virtuous Pandavas and the wicked Kauravas in which good overcomes evil. It includes the Bhagavad Gita.
Bhagavad Gita:	"The Song of the Lord", spoken by Krishna. This is the most important scripture for many Hindus. It is considered an Upanishad.
Ramayana:	epic telling of Rama and Sita
Manusmriti:	The Laws of Manu: an ancient and important text on dharma, including personal and social laws
Sanskrit:	sacred language of the Hindu scriptures
Sutra:	short saying or verse

CONCEPTS

The four aims in life

Dharma:	religious duty, righteousness
Artha:	economic development, material success, for good of family and society
Kama:	enjoyment of the senses
Moksha:	liberation from the continuous cycle of birth, death, and rebirth
Ahimsa:	non-violence, respect for life
Seva:	service, either to God or to humanity

KEY BELIEFS

Brahman:	Ultimate Reality, the Supreme Spirit, the Infinite, God – that from which everything arises and into which everything will dissolve
Atman:	eternal self; the soul of the individual
Trimurti:	the three aspects of the Godhead – Brahma, the Creator; Vishnu, the Saviour and Preserver; and Shiva, the Lord of Destruction and Recreation
Avatar:	descent; God taking form and coming to earth
Reincarnation:	rebirth of the soul

CONCEPTS

Karma:	actions and the effects of actions; the law of cause and effect
Samsara:	the continuous cycle of birth, death, and rebirth in the world
Nirvana:	state of peace; the ceasing of material existence
Bhakti yoga:	the path of loving devotion – one of several paths to moksha and union with God
Karma yoga:	one of several paths to moksha and union with God. It involves acting without any selfish desires.
Jnana yoga:	the path of knowledge, another path to moksha and union with God. It involves devoting one's whole life to study, yoga, and meditation.
Raja yoga:	a path to moksha and union with God, involving self-control and meditation

Understanding Islam

Islam means submission or obedience. It has the same root of letters as – and thus a similar meaning to – the Arabic word for peace (salam). Submission means acceptance of God's commands and obedience is putting them into practice. Submission and obedience to the will of God lead to peace. The religion of Islam is based on belief in one God, Allah. The oneness (tawhid) of God is complete.

Origins

Islam, according to Muslims, is the original true religion, given to Adam at the beginning of time. Through the ages, God has revealed His guidance to his messengers (prophets) Abraham, Moses, and others. The Prophet Muhammad was the last prophet to receive the message of Allah. The final and complete revelation that he received from God was written down to form the Qur'an.

The Prophet Muhammad was born in 571 CE in Makkah. His father died before he was born and his mother died when he was six, and so he was brought up by his uncle. He looked after his uncle's sheep and later worked in the family business. He was respected in the community and became known as "the Trustworthy". Muhammad worked for a wealthy business woman called Khadijah and made a success of her trading company. She proposed to him and they were married.

Muhammad was disturbed by the selfish and corrupt way of life of the Makkans. He was particularly distressed by the worship of idols at the House of God, the Ka'bah. He would go into the mountains to pray and meditate. It was on one of these occasions, in the month of Ramadan in the year 610 CE, that he first heard the angel Jibril: "Read in the name of your Lord who created. Created man from a clot of blood; Read, your Lord is most Generous; Who taught by the pen; Taught man what he did not know." [Qur'an, 96: 1-5]. This marked the beginning of the Prophet Muhammad's role as Allah's messenger. Over a period of 23 years the Prophet received the complete and final revelation of Allah.

The Prophet Muhammad began to preach Allah's message in Makkah. However, the Makkans persecuted him and his followers. He accepted an invitation to go to Madinah to help settle disputes in the community there. At Madinah the Prophet was able to found a Muslim community (the ummah) and establish a way of life based on the teachings of Islam.

The life of the ummah was built on five practices, known as the Pillars of Islam. The first is Shahadah, the declaration that there is no God but Allah and that Muhammad is his messenger. The second pillar is Salah, set prayer five times a day. Fasting during the month of Ramadan is the third pillar. The fourth is Zakah, giving to the poor and needy. The last of the five pillars is Hajj, which is pilgrimage to Makkah at least once in a lifetime.

The Makkans did not cooperate with the Prophet Muhammad and would not allow his followers to enter Makkah on pilgrimage. They even sent armies to try to overthrow him. However, eventually, the Prophet approached Makkah with a vast army of followers. The Makkans let him into the city, and he was able to establish the way of Islam, cleanse the Ka'bah of idols, and dedicate the building to the one true God, Allah.

Ethics

Muslims believe that men and women have free will. They are free to follow their own selfish desires or to follow the straight path laid down in the Qur'an. Muslims also believe that, on the Day of Judgement, everyone will be judged according to his or her actions. Those who have followed the straight path will enjoy everlasting life in Paradise.

Activity Sheet	Key concept	Objective for students
4.1 Some Key Beliefs in Islam	Allah, tawhid, Akhirah, prophets, Ummah	To gain understanding of these key beliefs in Islam.
4.2 The Straight Path	The Qur'an as a guide, zakah, Ramadan fast	To learn about some of the ethical teachings of Islam.
4.3 The Importance of Prayer	Prayer (salah)	To understand the central importance of prayer in Islam.
4.4 Thinking through Islam	Revision task	To revise key words and concepts in Islam.

Some Key Beliefs in Islam

Allah

There is no picture or symbol to represent Allah. It is forbidden to try to create an image of Allah. However, there are ninety-nine names for God which help Muslims understand the nature of Allah: for example, the Most Merciful, the Most Kind, the All-knowing, the All-powerful, the Most Wise, the Creator. Some Muslims recite the ninety-nine names as an act of worship, using prayer beads.

1 Find out about the names of Allah. Choose six of the names and explain what they tell you about the Islamic belief in God.

Tawhid, the oneness of God

Belief in tawhid, the oneness of God, is central to Islam. The teachings of the Qur'an reject the Christian idea of the Trinity – God as Three in One. Muslims believe that to suggest that God had a son is to deny the oneness of God.

2 Write a conversation in which a Muslim and a Christian share their views about God.

Akhirah, life after death

Muslims believe in life after death – Akhirah. This belief gives life meaning: "Do you think then that we have created you for nothing and that you would not be returned to us?" [Qur'an, 23: 115].

3 Prepare for a classroom debate on the question of life after death and whether life has meaning without a belief in life after death. Include the Islamic point of view when you make your notes about different views in preparation for the debate.

Prophets

Muslims believe that Allah sent prophets (or messengers) in every age to guide men and women on the "straight path".

4 Find out about the lives of three prophets and write a short paragraph on each. Make sure that you give the Islamic account of the prophet rather than the biblical version. Report on your work to the rest of the class. Discuss some of the differences between the Islamic stories and the biblical versions.

The Ummah

The Prophet Muhammad set up the first Muslim community (ummah) at Madinah. This served as a model on which he was later able to build when he returned to Makkah.

5 Find out about the Prophet Muhummad's journey to Madinah in 622 CE, his time there, and his return to Makkah. Write up your findings in the form of a news article or radio report.

A sense of community

Muslims are encouraged to build a sense of community through praying together, coming together on Fridays at the mosque, sharing the fast of Ramadan, meeting for the festivals, and going on pilgrimage (Hajj).

6 What do you think builds a sense of community in a society? Which of the following would help and which would work against a sense of community? Sort these ideas into two columns and add some ideas of your own.

a) shared moral values;
b) an emphasis on personal ambition;
c) a shared vision for the future;
d) a society based on material wealth;
e) a sense of common purpose;
f) a lifestyle based on personal success;
g) opportunities for eating and celebrating together;
h) housing estates with no centre;
i) opportunities for meeting others, e.g. community centre;
j) tall blocks of flats;
k) shared history and culture;
l) television in every room;
m) shared entertainment, e.g. dancing, singing together;
n) everyone owning their own car;
o) shared transport system;
p) shopping on-line;
q) a market place and local shops;
r) leaders who simply want personal power;
s) leaders who are working for the common good.

The Straight Path

The Qur'an as a guide

Muslims believe that, on the Day of Judgement, everyone will be judged according to his or her actions in this life. Those who have followed the "Straight Path", as laid down in the Qur'an, will go to Paradise. The following teachings from the Qur'an indicate the "Straight Path":

"Be kind to your parents and the relatives and the orphans, and those in need and speak nicely to people." [2: 83]

"Practise forgiveness, command decency and avoid ignorant people." [7: 199]

"Have you seen him who rejects religion? That is the person who pushes the orphan aside and does not encourage feeding the needy." [107: 1-3]

"Whenever you speak, speak justly." [6: 152]

"Cooperate with one another for virtue and piety and do not cooperate with one another for sin and transgression." [5: 2]

"And give full measure when measuring out, and weigh with proper scales." [17: 35]

"If Allah is your helper none can overcome you and if He does not help you, who is there to help you?" [3: 160]

1 With a partner, discuss the meanings of the above quotations from the Qur'an. Then write a summary of what you think are the main characteristics of the Straight Path.

Zakah – giving to the poor

"Those who spend their wealth for the sake of Allah night and day, both privately and publicly, will get their reward from their Lord." [2: 274]

One of the Five Pillars of Islam is zakah – giving a percentage of your wealth to the poor and needy. It is not the same as charity because charity is voluntary; zakah is a religious requirement. However, paying zakah is not the same as paying a tax, because the money does not go to those in power to spend as they think fit; it goes to the poor and needy in the community.

2 Design a zakah collection box, using quotations from the Qur'an as part of the design, to encourage giving.

Some Hadith about giving

Hadith are sayings of the Prophet Muhammad, which were carefully collected after the Prophet's death. They are second in authority to the Qur'an. Here are some examples of Hadith on the subject of giving:

"Every single day each person has two angels near him who have descended from heaven. The one says, 'O God, compensate the person who gives charity.' The other says, 'O God, inflict a loss on the person who withholds his money.'"

"Spend generously and do not keep an account; God will keep an account for you."

"Avoid hell by giving to charity, even if it means sharing your last date, and, if you have nothing at all, by speaking a kind word."

"Wealth does not consist in the abundance of possessions. Wealth is wealth of the soul."

3 Discuss the meaning of these Hadith, and use them to prepare a sermon that might be given at the mosque to encourage Muslims to give generously.

The Ramadan fast

It was in the month of Ramadan that the Prophet Muhammad received the revelations from Allah, which became the words of the Qur'an. For Muslims, Ramadan is therefore a time of thanksgiving for the gift of the Qur'an.

For the whole month, they fast during daylight hours. Fasting requires self-discipline. It is a way to build up the strength of character needed to overcome temptation and evil. It is also a way of shifting one's thoughts away from shopping and preparing food to more spiritual matters. The experience of fasting with others draws the Islamic community together; there is a sense of being one in the testing time of the fast. The fast of Ramadan is also regarded as an act of worship: the Muslim is putting the will of Allah before personal greed and physical satisfaction.

4 Find out more about the fast of Ramadan and the festival of Eid-ul-Fitr that follows it. Write a report on Ramadan and Eid-ul-Fitr for a newspaper. Explain the meaning of the fast for Muslims.

The Importance of Prayer

Daily words

The following are some of the words said by Muslims each time they pray, at each of the five set prayer times every day.

"All praise is for Allah, the Lord of the Universe, the most Merciful, the most Kind; Master of the day of judgement. You alone we worship, from You alone we seek help. Guide us along the straight path – the path of those whom You favoured, not of those who earned Your anger or went astray."

1 What are the beliefs expressed in this prayer? What do we learn about the Muslim view of God? Answer these questions in writing.

The Prophet Muhammad's Farewell

In his last sermon, the Prophet Muhammad called on Muslims to hold fast to the teachings of the Qur'an and to follow his example. He recited these words from the Qur'an: "This day I have perfected your religion for you and completed my favour onto you and have chosen for you Islam as a religion." [5: 3]. Many Muslims wept when they heard this because they understood that the Prophet was saying that his work on earth was nearly complete and that he would soon die.

The Prophet continued to lead the Muslims in prayer, right up until shortly before his death. Even during his final few days of illness he appeared at the mosque while the prayers were in progress. The Muslims present were overjoyed to see him and wanted him to lead prayers. However, he was too weak and he returned to his house where he lay down beside his wife and recited the words: "With those upon whom God has showered His Favour, the prophets and the saints and the martyrs and the good, and they are the best of companions." [4: 69]

2 What does this story tell you about the importance of prayer to the Prophet Muhammad?

Personal prayer

As well as saying set prayers five times a day, Muslims must also perform du'a – personal prayer. They ask Allah for guidance in times of difficulty or for forgiveness. They may also pray for family or for those in need. The Prophet Muhammad promised that Allah listens:

"Our Lord (glorified and exalted be he) descends each night to the Earth's sky when there remains the final third of the night and he says: 'Who is saying a prayer [du'a] to me that I may answer it? Who is asking something of me that I may give it him? Who is asking forgiveness of me that I may forgive him?'" [Hadith]

3 What things do you think a Muslim might pray for today? Who are the people with the greatest troubles and greatest needs today? Discuss your answers in class. Put together a class list.

Thinking through Islam

Revision Task

In groups choose one of the boxes. Prepare and present a short talk explaining the words in your box. Use your notes and information in the *Thinking Through Religion* textbook to help you. You might also present pictures to illustrate the meanings of the words.

CONCEPTS

Islam:	the peace that comes from submitting to God
Ummah:	community of Muslims; the nation of Islam
Salam:	peace, in Arabic
Ibadah:	faith in action/worship
Jihad:	struggle against evil (Greater Jihad, Lesser Jihad)
Shari'ah:	Islamic law

CONCEPTS

Angels:	beings created by Allah from light; they have no free will and are completely obedient to Allah
Khalifah:	agent or someone trusted by Allah to carry out His will on earth and be His representative
Mosque:	place of prostration, place of worship
Jumu'ah:	Friday prayers
Du'a:	personal prayer

MORALITY

Submission:	acceptance of and obedience to God's will
Shari'ah:	Islamic law based upon the Qur'an and Sunnah
Haram:	forbidden, unlawful
Halal:	lawful and permitted
Sadaqah:	voluntary payment for charity
Zakat-ul-Fitr:	payment of zakah at the Eid-ul-Fitr festival at the end of Ramadan

THE FIVE PILLARS

Shahadah:	declaration of faith: There is no God but Allah and Muhammad is his prophet
Salah:	set prayer, five times a day
Sawm:	fasting during the month of Ramadan
Zakah:	giving to the poor and needy
Hajj:	pilgrimage to Makkah at least once in lifetime

HOLY BOOKS

Qur'an:	the holy scripture of Islam; the revelations of Allah to the Prophet Muhammad
Surah:	chapter of the Qur'an
Hadith:	saying(s) of the Prophet Muhammad – a major source of Islamic law
Sunnah:	the "well-trodden path" or example; model practices, customs, and traditions of the Prophet Muhammad. The Hadith and the Sirah make up the Sunnah.
Sirah:	biographical writings about the conduct and example of the Prophet Muhammad

KEY BELIEFS

Allah:	God, in Arabic; the word is singular and has no gender attached to it
Tawhid:	the oneness/unity of God/Allah
Al-Qadr:	Allah's complete and final control over the fulfilment of events or destiny; nothing can happen without the will of Allah
Akhirah:	eternal life after death
Barzakh:	a state of waiting until the Day of Judgement
Risalah:	prophethood, channel of communication between Allah and humankind

Understanding Judaism

The name "Judaism" was not used until the beginning of the Christian era, at the end of the 1st century BCE [2 Maccabees 2: 21; 8: 1; 14: 38]. It is a name which refers variously to *people with a shared genealogy* (a Jewish person is identified as s/he who has a Jewish mother, and a history which goes back to "our fathers Abraham, Isaac, and Jacob") and to *people who follow God's laws* as revealed in the Torah.

Today especially, a distinction is often made between "cultural" and "religious" Judaism. Cultural (or secular) Jews accept the culture and values of Judaism but do not necessarily keep the laws as laid down in the Torah. Cultural Jews will keep such traditions as the Shabbat and different parts of the kashrut (food laws). Even the most secular of Jews will attend the synagogue on Yom Kippur. "Religious" Jews try to keep all of God's laws as laid down in their holy book, the Torah. But even then there are differences between Orthodox, Reform, Conservative, Progressive, Reconstructionist, and Liberal Judaism as to how the laws are interpreted.

Although Judaism is sometimes perceived as a religion preoccupied with law, it is not legalistic. Rather, the Torah is "a language of love, a way of saying 'Yes' to God". [J. Bowker ed., *Oxford Dictionary of World Religions*]

Clearly there is no normative definition of Judaism. But, as far as the Jewish people are concerned, it is impossible to be a Jew and also a member of another religion. Therefore, Jewish Christians (also referred to as "messianic Jews" – those who accept Jesus Christ to be the Messiah) are not accepted as Jews by Jews in general.

Origins

With the term Judaism not being used until the end of the 1st century BCE, the question of when Judaism actually began is answered in a number of ways. Some trace the beginnings of the religion to God's call of Abraham (about 18 centuries BCE), who is claimed to be the ancestor of the Jewish people. Others trace the beginnings of Judaism as we know it to Moses receiving the Torah at Mount Sinai (around 13 centuries BCE). Others trace the beginnings of modern-day Judaism to the time when the Talmud was completed – the time of the Jewish sages (about 500 CE).

Today's Judaism differs in many ways from the biblical religion. For example, many Jews today believe in a life after death, although this idea does not appear clearly in the Tenakh. Original ethical teachings such as "an eye for an eye" are no longer practised. What can be said is that Jewish roots can be traced to biblical times. When many people talk about Judaism they refer to "rabbinic Judaism", the way of life set down by the rabbis from the 2nd century CE onwards. This rabbinic Judaism is the foundation for the various groups within Judaism today.

"There is not now, and never has been, a single Judaism . . . Each took shape in its own circumstances and in response to its own political and social issues. But all Judaisms have recapitulated that single paradigmatic experience of the Torah of 'Moses' . . . While Jewish history records a variety of competing Judaisms . . . a single Judaism predominated, the Judaism of the dual Torah, both written and oral. This Judaism is called, variously, 'rabbinic', after its principal authorities; 'talmudic', after its authoritative document; . . . or simply Judaism." [J. Z. Smith ed., *The Harper Collins Dictionary of Religion*, 1996]

Activity Sheet	Key concept	Objective for students
5.1 Tempers flare over Shabbat	The holiness of Shabbat	To learn about the importance of Shabbat for religious Jews and to consider to what extent religious regulations should govern a country.
5.2 Is that a deal?	Yom Kippur and forgiveness	To learn about the meaning of the Jewish fast, Yom Kippur, and reflect upon the relationship between God and humanity.
5.3 Thinking through Judaism	Revision task	To revise key words and concepts in Judaism.

Tempers flare over Shabbat

Secular and religious demonstrators fight over opening of Drugstore on Shabbat

RELIGIOUS Israeli Jews and secular demonstrators gathered on Saturday afternoon outside Jerusalem's Drugstore 2000. It was open for the first time on Shabbat. Earlier on in the day the owners of the store were fined two and a half thousand pounds for violating work and rest hour laws.

The new store, also selling different foods, opened despite a number of telephone threats from religious Israelis. Throughout the morning the store was crowded, but by mid-afternoon religious demonstrators came to protest – shouting "Shabbat". At one point a fist-fight broke out. Police separated the people and broke up the fight.

Groups of secular Israelis gathered outside the store, arguing with religious Israelis about the role of religion in Israel. Should religious laws govern everyday activities like shopping? Virtually all shops and cinemas close for the whole of the Shabbat, bringing Jerusalem to a standstill.

The demonstrations over the opening of Drugstore 2000 are part of a larger battle over the soul of Jerusalem. During the last six months secular and religious Jews have been flexing their muscles over the opening of a number of restaurants and shops throughout the city.

The harediim [religious Jews] believe that God's words in the Torah must be obeyed. One of the Ten Commandments clearly states that on the Sabbath "no one is to work" [Exodus 20]. The secular Jews believe that in a free country all people should be allowed to live as they wish. A 55-year-old mother of four bought some pasta and sauce: "We didn't really need anything," she admitted. "We only came to show support."

Abergil, who owns a small round-the-clock store in one of Jerusalem's neighbourhoods, said: "I have a right to live my life without them imposing on me."

Avraham Poraz, a politician, was at the store: "This time they won't get away with it. If they try to close the store, we will make sure it stays open." Commenting that in Europe stores are open on Sundays, he went on to say, "We have to hope that the harediim will understand the needs of the secular public in Jerusalem."

[Jerusalem Post, City Notes "In Jerusalem", 26 February 1999]

Q

1 Why are the religious and secular Jews in Jerusalem coming to blows?

2 Why do religious Jews regard the Shabbat as important?

3 Explain how the observance of Shabbat traditions may help to preserve Jewish unity.

4 What are the advantages and disadvantages of a country being run according to religious laws?

5 What do you think are the advantages of keeping a special day?

Is that a deal?

It was the eve of Yom Kippur. It had been a rushed day. She had spent the morning cooking for supper before the day-long fast began and for the feast which would break the fast the following evening. At midday she had gone around to say sorry to her parents – sorry for all the things which had come in the way of their relationship during the last year. She had already made peace with her children and husband. She just had enough time for a bath before her husband and children came home. At the end of supper, when the table was cleared, she lit the candles and said the blessing for the Day of Atonement.

Yom Kippur was a good day – a chance to be especially close to God, to forgive others, and to be forgiven by them in return. She had prepared well, and had done all that was humanly possible. When she arrived at the synagogue it was already crowded. On this one day of the year the whole community met to seek God's forgiveness for sins committed in the past year. There was a certain mystery and awe on Yom Kippur – an expectation that God would be kind and merciful.

The congregation began to sing and pray: "For the sins we have committed . . ." She started to think of all the things that had gone wrong over the last year:

"What a miserable person I am . . .
I could have been a better wife . . .
I could have given more to people in need . . .
I could have given more time to my children . . .
I could have been kinder . . .
I lose my temper far too often . . . "

As she continued to think about her life, tears came to her eyes.

"Dear God, please forgive me, you who are so . . . Come to think of it God, you haven't had such a good year yourself! The world is in such a mess, and a lot of it is down to you. There was that massive earthquake in Mexico killing thousands . . . and what about that volcano which erupted in the Caribbean, crushing whole communities . . . that old man battered to death in his own flat . . . that terrible plane crash in Russia . . . the thousands of homeless people who have to sleep rough night after night. Think of all the happiness you could have created and didn't. Think of all the misery you could have stopped and didn't. It seems to me that you need as much forgiveness as I do! I'll tell you what . . . I am a reasonable woman – if you forgive me, I'll forgive you. Is that a deal?"

The woman in the seat behind her had heard everything. "Whatever are you saying? Don't you know who you are talking to? You had God really squirming in the palm of your hand. Why did you let God off so lightly?"

[adapted from "Give and Take" in A. Wood and R. Richardson, *Inside Stories*, Trentham Books, 1992]

1 How would you describe the relationship that the mother in this story has with God? What picture of God does she have?

2 Does she take her own wrongdoings seriously? Why do you think she blames God? Is she right to do so, or is she just shifting her own blame?

3 What deal does she make with God? Does she have a right to make a deal with God? What does the story teach you about the nature of covenants (agreements) with God?

Thinking through Judaism

Revision Task

In groups choose one of the boxes. Prepare and present a short talk explaining the words in your box. Use your notes and information in the *Thinking Through Religion* textbook to help you. You might also present pictures to illustrate the meanings of the words.

CONCEPTS

Shema:	central Jewish prayer affirming belief in one God
Covenant:	agreement, between God and humanity
Kashrut:	food laws
Shabbat:	day of rest, starting at sunset on Friday and ending at nightfall on Saturday
Yom Kippur:	Day of Atonement

KEY BELIEFS

One God

Shekinah:	the divine presence
Teshuva:	penitence, returning to God
Tikkun Olam:	care for the world and the environment

HOLY BOOKS

Tenakh:	the collected 24 books of the Jewish Bible
Torah:	law, teaching; the Five Books of Moses
Mishnah:	the first writing down of the Oral Tradition, about 200 CE
Talmud:	"study": a collection of writings, completed in 500 CE, based on rabbis' discussions about right and wrong. Mishnah and Gemara (commentary on the Mishnah) collected together

MORALITY

Ten Sayings:	Ten Commandments which God gave Moses
Mitzvot:	613 commandments contained in the Torah
Halakhah:	"path" or "way", from root meaning "to walk"; the code of conduct comprising all aspects of Jewish life
Kosher:	allowed
Treif:	prohibited
Tzedakah:	righteousness; an act of charity

Understanding Sikhism

Origins

Sikhism is the youngest of the world's six main religions today. Its followers trace their tradition back to the lives of ten Gurus, the first of whom was Guru Nanak. Nanak was born in 1469 in the village of Talwandi in the Punjab region of India (now in Pakistan). His family was Hindu, but he grew up in an environment where those in power were Muslims. The influences of both Hinduism and Islam can be traced in the teachings of Guru Nanak. However, Sikhism is more than a mixture of these two religions. Guru Nanak's teaching has its basis in a religious experience in which the Guru claimed that he stood in the presence of God.

Guru Nanak had no time for hypocrisy, meaningless ritual, and superstition. He was impatient with religious leaders who seemed to put obstacles in the way of true devotion rather than helping people to find God. A life of prayer, meditation, and devotion to God led him to seek the truth that lay beyond the outward forms of religion. His message was: "There is no Muslim, there is no Hindu, we are all children of God." Guru Nanak preached this message throughout India. He eventually settled in Kartarpur and established a way of life based on belief in the oneness of God and the equality of all people.

By setting up this community, Guru Nanak ensured that his work continued after his death; and by appointing Guru Angad to be the Guru after him, he guaranteed a leader for the community. In all there were ten living Gurus:

Guru Nanak	1469-1539
Guru Angad	1504-1552
Guru Amar Das	1479-1574
Guru Ram Das	1534-1581
Guru Arjan	1563-1606
Guru Hargobind	1595-1644
Guru Har Rai	1630-1661
Guru Har Krishan	1656-1664
Guru Tegh Bahadur	1621-1675
Guru Gobind Singh	1666-1708

The tenth Guru, Guru Gobind Singh, saw the need to unite the Sikh community in the face of persecution. In 1699, when Sikhs had gathered in Anandpur for Baisakhi (new year), he founded the Khalsa, the community of initiated Sikhs. He established the five Ks and a moral code for members of the Khalsa. In this way he ensured that the Sikhs would be fit to meet the challenges that lay ahead.

Scriptures

The hymns of Guru Nanak and the words of the other Gurus were treasured and collected over many years. They formed the text of the Guru Granth Sahib, the holy scripture of the Sikhs. The Guru Granth Sahib also contains the words of Muslim and Hindu religious teachers. Guru Gobind Singh instructed Sikhs from his death onwards to treat the Guru Granth Sahib as their living Guru.

Sikh belief is summed up in the Mool Mantra (the opening words of the Guru Granth Sahib): " There is one and only One God; Truth is his name; He is the Creator; He is without fear; He is without hate; Immortal; He is beyond birth and death; he is self-illuminated; He is realised by the Grace of the Guru." Sikhs today try to follow the way of life established by the Gurus, based on the unity of God and the equality of all.

Activity Sheet	Key concept	Objective for students
6.1 The Khalsa	The Khalsa and equality	To learn about the importance of the Khalsa for Sikhs around the world, and to consider the ideal of equality and how it applies today.
6.2 Wearing the Kirpan	Keeping one's religion in adversity	To consider two individual experiences of Sikhs in the West, and think about the right to religious self-expression.
6.3 Sikh Morality	Morality	To learn about the importance of honesty, service, and dependence on God in Sikhism.
6.4 Thinking through Sikhism	Revision task	To revise key words and concepts in Sikhism.

The Khalsa

The greatest of days for Sikhs was the day when the tenth Guru, Guru Gobind Singh, created the Khalsa (the Sikh community) – 13 April 1699. This activity sheet explores the importance of the Khalsa for Sikhs.

In 1999 the 300th anniversary of the founding of the Khalsa was celebrated all over the world.

Worldwide Celebrations Mark the Founding of the Khalsa

MILLIONS of Sikhs across India today are celebrating the 300th anniversary of the formal founding of the Sikh brotherhood, as the community, challenged by modernity, strives to keep alive the traditions of the country's youngest religion.

Up to five million devotees, including Sikhs from abroad, are expected to gather at the white marble Keshgarh Sahib Gurdwara, or Sikh temple, at Anandpur Sahib, to celebrate the raising of the Khalsa in 1699.

Langars – free kitchens – served food to devotees en route while army bands from the Sikh regimental centre and the Punjab state police played Punjabi tunes.

[By Rahul Bedi in New Delhi, India, *Daily Telegraph*, 14 April 1999]

A speech in London

In London, one celebration of the anniversary took place at the Royal Albert Hall on 25 April 1999. The British Home Secretary, Jack Straw, addressed the audience. He congratulated the Sikhs on the 300th anniversary of the formation of the Khalsa. His speech was set in the context of a bombing that had occurred in Brick Lane (the heart of London's Bangladeshi community) the previous day. Mr Straw stated that the principles of justice and freedom, which the Khalsa hold dear, would be upheld in bringing those responsible for the bombings to justice.

Sikhs mark 300 years with swords and lasers

Priests are chanting prayers at the temple, brightly illuminated by rainbow coloured laser lights, and elaborately turbaned swordsmen, portraying Sikhism's militaristic traditions, are preparing to participate in a massive parade through Anandpur Sahib on horses and chariots.

[By Rahul Bedi in New Delhi, India, *Daily Telegraph*, 13 April 1999]

1 Look again at the story of Guru Gobind Singh setting up the Khalsa (see page 77 of *Thinking Through Religion*). Tell the story in the form of a newspaper article. Make sure you discuss the possible reasons for the events of Baisakhi 1699: say why Guru Gobind Singh felt it was time to prepare the Sikhs in this way, and which values the Khalsa holds dear.

2 The Khalsa is the community of initiated Sikhs. Read the words here, which are said at the initiation ceremony, and find out more about what happens at this ceremony (the Amrit ceremony) and about the promises that Sikhs make on the occasion. Write a report of your findings.

WORDS SPOKEN AT THE SIKH INITIATION CEREMONY

"As from today you are born to the Guru and freed from rebirth. You are now a member of the Khalsa. Guru Gobind Singh is your spiritual father ... Because you are all children of the same father you are spiritual brothers, one with another and with all others who have received the amrit initiation. This means you should put aside all concern for caste, status, birth, country and religion, for you are now exclusively a member of the sublime Khalsa. You must worship God alone, spurning all other gods, goddesses, incarnations and prophets. You must accept the ten Gurus and their teachings as your only means of deliverance." [Rahit Maryada]

3 The Sikh community is based upon the ideal of the equality of all people, leading to justice and tolerance towards all people. Do you think this Khalsa ideal is a practical way of living in today's world?

Wearing the Kirpan

1 Read the following two news stories – one from the USA, the other from England. What are the issues involved?

Sikh priest faces prosecution for wearing a kirpan

Recently a Sikh priest was arrested in Mentor, Ohio, on charges of carrying a concealed weapon.

On the way back to his home in Cleveland, the 69-year-old Gurbachan Singh Bhatia was involved in a minor traffic accident. During interrogation the police found a 6-inch sheathed knife under his tunic. Despite his pleas that he is an initiated Sikh and that he is required to carry a knife as part of his religion, he was arrested. He is to appear in court this week and, if convicted, the elderly priest could be sentenced to six months in jail and fined up to $1,000.

In a multicultural and multireligious society, certain genuine beliefs can run afoul of the law. To be different does not mean threatening. One man's religious symbol is not another man's threatening weapon.

A lack of sensitivity and understanding can lead to the clash of cultures as it did in Mentor. The police could have issued the priest a licence to carry his beloved knife. Instead they ended up humiliating him and his faith.

[by Preet Mohan S. Ahluwalia, Sikhnet, from *Akron Beacon Journal*, Sunday, 19 September 1999]

Lord Irvine apologises to Sikh for dagger ban

THE Lord Chancellor has apologised to a Sikh solicitor whose ceremonial dagger was confiscated as he entered the High Court.

Arup Singh Choudry was ordered to surrender his kirpan in May after the weapon was picked up by the court's metal detectors, despite Lord Irvine of Lairg's instruction to court staff that they should respect Sikh traditional dress.

Although Mr Choudry frequently did business at the High Court, this was the first time he had worn the kirpan since being baptised into the Sikh faith at the age of 49. Mr Choudry said: "I wasn't wearing it to threaten anybody. It is for self-defence or the defence of others. It is our symbol of righteousness and justice. I was asked to leave it at security. I was sensible about this and complied before complaining afterwards."

Under guidance issued by Lord Irvine two years ago, Sikhs are allowed to bring their kirpans into court as long as the daggers are no longer than six inches. In his letter to Mr Choudry, Lord Irvine wrote: "I can only apologise for the problems which you have experienced at the Royal Court of Justice and for any embarrassment caused. I have asked my officials to make sure that all courts are reminded of the current policy."

Earlier this week Mr Choudry was able to enter the Palace of Westminster with his kirpan, but on aircraft he normally leaves the knife in his luggage.

[By David Millward , Thursday, 1 July 1999, copyright of Telegraph Group Limited 1999]

2 Why do Sikhs wear the kirpan? What does it symbolise?

3 These two stories show two different reactions. Who acted appropriately in these two stories?

4 Should a government have a right to limit a person's religious self-expression?

Sikh Morality: honesty, service, and dependence on God

Q

1 The Sikh Gurus said that all Sikhs must earn an honest living. What do you think is meant by this? Which kinds of ways of earning a living could be seen as honest and which might be regarded as not honest? Look at the following ways of earning a living and discuss them in pairs: nurse; road sweeper; thief; politician; teacher; worker in arms factory; journalist; banker; estate agent; solicitor; shopkeeper; gardener; waitress/waiter.

2 Sikhs are required to share their wealth with others. What are the different ways in which people can be said to possess riches? Write down ten ways in which people are fortunate. Suggest ways in which the riches they have can be shared in the community. For example, someone might be rich in knowledge: how might they share their wealth in the community?

Haumai

"Get a life!"; "Be yourself!"; "Pull yourself together!" Sayings such as these suggest that we are in control and that we can get on in life without any help. Sikhs believe that this sense of self-reliance – haumai – is wrong. Haumai is thinking that we do not need God; it is pride and arrogance. Sikhs believe that we depend on God for everything: the air we breathe, the food we eat, even the life within us. It is therefore wrong to forget how much we depend on God and his goodness.

3 Draw a diagram/cartoon/symbol to illustrate the Sikh view of haumai and the importance of recognising dependence on God.

4 Explain what the story of Guru Nanak choosing his successor teaches Sikhs about (a) hard work; (b) pride; (c) the Sikh community; (d) service.

GURU NANAK CHOOSES HIS SUCCESSOR

Guru Nanak was getting old and looking for someone who would continue his work. One day he was working with friends on the farmland. It was late and there was hay grass to carry home. He called his two sons to him and said: "Please would you carry this grass home."

His sons refused: "We do not really need it and anyway it is dirty and it will spoil our clothes. Ask one of your Sikhs to do it for you."

"The Sikh and the son are equal before God," said the Guru. "You must work as hard as anyone else."

The Guru turned to his Sikhs and a man called Lehna ran to help the Guru and carried the grass home without complaint. Guru Nanak saw that he could not depend on his sons to continue his work. So he made Lehna his successor and called him Angad.

Thinking through Sikhism

Revision Task

In groups choose one of the boxes. Prepare and present a short talk explaining the words in your box. Use your notes and information in the *Thinking Through Religion* textbook to help you. You might also present pictures to illustrate the meanings of the words.

CONCEPTS

Sikh: disciple, seeker, one who follows the teachings of the ten Gurus and the Guru Granth Sahib

Guru: spiritual teacher – used only for the ten human Gurus and the Guru Granth Sahib

Langar: Guru's kitchen; refers to the gurdwara dining hall and to the food served in it

Gurdwara: the house of the Guru, Sikh place of worship

KEY BELIEFS

Mool Mantra: credal statement about God; the basic statement of teaching at the beginning of the Guru Granth Sahib

Ik Onkar: "There is only One God" – the first phrase of the Mool Mantra. The Gurmukhi script for this phrase has become a Sikh symbol known as the Ik Onkar.

Akal Purakh: "the eternal one" – a name often used for God

Sikh: learner, disciple; a person who follows the teachings of the ten Gurus and the Guru Granth Sahib

Khalsa: Sikh community, community of the pure

THE FIVE Ks

Kes: uncut hair

Kangha: comb, worn in the hair

Kara: steel bangle, worn on right wrist

Kachera: shorts worn as underwear

Kirpan: sword

HOLY BOOKS

Guru Granth Sahib: collection of Sikh scriptures, first compiled by Guru Arjan (as the Adi Granth), and given its formal form by Guru Gobind Singh

Akhand Path: continuous reading of the Guru Granth Sahib from beginning to end

Japji Sahib: a morning prayer, composed by Guru Nanak, which forms the first chapter of the Guru Granth Sahib

Rahit Maryada: Sikh code of discipline

Gurmukhi: the script of the Punjabi language in which the scriptures are written

MORALITY

Hukam: God's will/command

Haumai: self-reliance – forgetting that we depend on God for everything; egoism. It is a major spiritual defect and cause of suffering.

Kurahit: prohibitions, e.g. intoxicants

Sewa: service to others – an essential part of the life of every Sikh

Vand chhakna: sharing one's time, talents, and earnings with the less fortunate

Kirat Karni: earning one's living by one's own honest efforts – one of the three rules by which Sikhs try to live their lives

Questions of Meaning

Chapters 7, 8, and 9 in Part B of *Thinking Through Religion* address some fundamental questions. Is there a God? Why do people suffer? Is there a life after death? These questions are essentially spiritual. Students are encouraged to learn from the teachings of the religions and so come to a better understanding of their own approach to the issues. The chapters explore the following topics:

Does God Exist?
- The nature of God
- The nature of belief – the differing ways in which religions understand belief in God
- The nature of revelation (through holy books, personal experience, God intervening in history)
- The use of symbolic language to describe God
- Arguments leading to belief (e.g. design in universe, first cause, answered prayer, miracles, etc.)
- Arguments leading to non-belief (e.g. suffering, unanswered prayer, rationalism, etc.)

What about suffering?
- Types and origins of suffering
- The nature of human good and evil
- The problem of suffering for religious believers
- Divine goodness and supra-human evil
- The nature of God in relation to suffering
- Religious responses to suffering
- The purposes of suffering

Is there a life after death?
- Religious beliefs in life after death (including resurrection, heaven, hell, reincarnation, rebirth)
- Evidence for belief in life after death
- The relationship between behaviour in this life and existence afterwards
- Beliefs in judgement after death for earthly action

Examination candidates will be expected to:
- identify, investigate, and be able to respond to the fundamental questions of life;
- have gained a knowledge and understanding of religious responses to these fundamental questions;
- show that they can make reasoned and informed judgements about religious, and where appropriate, other responses to these fundamental questions of meaning;
- support their answers with reference to the teachings and sacred texts of the religion(s) studied, where appropriate; and be aware of how religious leaders and other faith members have interpreted these texts in the light of contemporary life;
- be aware of how religious teachings affect behaviour.

Activity Sheet/Study Skills Sheet	Key concept for students to consider
7.1 The Nature of God	Beliefs about the nature of God, from quotations from five world religions.
7.2 The Blind Men and the Elephant	Are all religions worshipping the same God? Why do religions differ?
7.3 Arguments for the existence of God	Cosmological, ontological, and moral arguments for the existence of God.
7.4 Angels	Are angels evidence of a supernatural realm and of God's existence?
7.5 Religious Experience and Revelation	What is a religious experience? Some individual personal accounts.
7.6 Exam Questions and Answers*	Sample questions and graded answers on the Existence of God.
8.1 Suffering: What the Religions Say	Quotations about suffering from six world religions.
8.2 A Letter from God	Is there a purpose in suffering?
8.3 "God will save us"	Where is God when people suffer? How does God send help?
8.4 Exam Questions and Answers*	Sample questions and graded answers on Suffering and Evil.
9.1 Life after Death: What the Religions Say	Quotations about life after death from six world religions.
9.2 Attitudes to Death	Examples of some individual people's attitudes to death.
9.3 Reincarnation Row	Understandings of reincarnation.
9.4 Exam Questions and Answers*	Sample questions and graded answers on Life after Death.

See Grade Descriptions on page 124.

48

The Nature of God

1 Make a list of the beliefs about God which are contained in these statements and quotations.

2 (a) What understandings about God do the religions of the world share?
(b) How do the religions differ from each other in their understandings about God?

3 Discuss whether the religions of the world believe in different gods or whether they believe in the same God but have different understandings of God's nature.

CHRISTIANITY

God is Creator and Sustainer; immanent; three in one; forgiving. Jesus was God incarnate.

"I believe in God, the Father Almighty, Maker of Heaven and earth." [Apostles' Creed]

"God is not far from any of us. 'We live in him. We walk in him. We are in him.'" [Acts 17: 28]

"Behold I stand at the door and knock; if any one hears My voice and opens the door, I will come in to him and eat with him, and he with Me." [Revelation 3: 20]

"Go ... teach all nations, baptising them in the name of the Father, and of the Son, and of the Holy Ghost." [Matthew 28: 19-20]

"The Word [of God] became a human being and ... lived among us. We saw his glory." [John 1: 14]

"He rescued us from the domain of darkness and brought us into the kingdom of his dear Son, through whom our release is secured and our sins are forgiven." [Colossians 1: 13-14]

HINDUISM

God is Creator; God is immanent:

"I am the father of this world, the mother, the establisher, the grandsire." [Bhagavad Gita, teachings of Krishna]

"The Lord lives in the heart of every creature ... Take refuge utterly in Him. By His grace you will find supreme peace, and the state which is beyond all change." [Bhagavad Gita 18: 61-62]

"I am the nucleus of every creature ... for without Me nothing can exist." [Bhagavad Gita 10: 39-41]

"From a very early period a Hindu was conscious of the fact that the multitudinous deities of his pantheon really illustrate the various ways of describing one single God, the eternally existent One Being with his manifold attributes and manifestations." [Jatindranath Banerjea, 1877-1930, "The Hindu Concept of God"]

Continued

ISLAM

Allah is perfect; Creator and Sustainer; transcendent; immanent; forgiving:

"He is God; there is no god but He. He is the Knower of the unseen and the visible. He is the All-merciful, the All-compassionate." [Qur'an, 59: 22]

"We indeed created man; and We know what his Soul whispers within him, and We are nearer to him than the jugular vein." [Qur'an, 50: 16]

"No vision can grasp Him, but His grasp is over all vision; He is above all comprehension, yet is acquainted with all things." [Qur'an, 6: 103]

"In the name of God, Most Gracious, Most Merciful. Praise be to God, the Cherisher and Sustainer of the worlds; Most Gracious, Most Merciful; Lord of the Day of Judgement. Thee we do worship, and Thine aid we seek." [Qur'an, 1: 1-5]

"He is with you, wherever you are." [Qur'an, 57: 4]

"God forgives all sins: for He is Oft-forgiving, Most Merciful." [Qur'an, 39: 53]

JUDAISM

God is Creator and Sustainer; all-present; transcendent:

"In the beginning God created the heaven and the earth ... God created man in His image." [Genesis 1: 1 and 27]

"There is no place without the Shekinah [God's presence]." [Talmud]

"The Lord our God is one Lord: and thou shalt love the Lord thy God with all thy heart, and with all thy soul and with all thy might." [Deuteronomy 6: 4-5]

"You shall have no other gods besides me ... I tolerate no rivals." [Exodus 20: 3-5]

"The fear of the Lord is the beginning of wisdom." [Proverbs 9: 10]

"Holy, holy, holy is the Lord Almighty; the whole earth is full of His glory." [Isaiah 6: 3]

"I believe with perfect faith that the Creator, blessed be his name, is not a body, and that he is free from all accidents of matter, and that he has not any form whatsoever." [Maimonides, 1135-1204, Spanish Hebrew philosopher, "Thirteen Principles"]

SIKHISM

God is Creator and Sustainer; transcendent; immanent:

"You are the Creator, O Lord, the Unknowable. You created the Universe of diverse kinds, colours, and qualities. You know your own Creation. All this is your play." [Guru Granth Sahib]

"The world is a garden, the Lord is the gardener, cherishing all, none neglected." [Guru Granth Sahib]

"The limit of the secret of God's heart cannot be known." [Guru Granth Sahib]

"Burnt be the mouth that asserts the Lord takes birth. He is neither born nor dies; neither enters birth nor departs. All pervasive is Nanak's Lord." [Guru Granth Sahib]

"Deep within the self is the Light of God. It radiates throughout the expanse of His creation." [Guru Granth Sahib]

The Blind Men and the Elephant

Some people argue that no one religion contains the *whole* truth; each religion has been given just *a partial revelation* of what God or Ultimate Reality is. To illustrate this point, some people use the story of the Blind Men and the Elephant.

Six blind men set out on journeys to discover for themselves true knowledge. A wise teacher has told them all to search for a strange animal which is the source of wisdom. They know only that this animal is called an elephant. On their journeys, each man comes across the elephant and begins to touch it, in order to discover what the animal is like.

The first grabs hold of the elephant's leg and thinks that what he holds is like a tree trunk, firm and solid. He exclaims that the elephant is like a pillar.

The second takes hold of the elephant's ear, and decides that the elephant is like a ship's sail.

The third holds on to the elephant's tail and says that the elephant is like a rope.

The fourth claims the elephant to be like a huge snake. He has touched only the elephant's trunk.

The fifth strokes the elephant's tusk, and concludes that the elephant is smooth and sharp.

And the sixth holds the tongue and knows that the elephant is wet and warm.

When the six men consult each other, each has a different version of what the elephant is like. But none of them has gathered the *whole* truth about the animal, nor has any one of them discovered what gave life to the elephant. They have all developed *partial* views.

1 How does this story explain why different religions have different beliefs about what truth is?

2 Why do you think that religions often conflict with each other over the nature of God or Ultimate Reality?

3 Do you think that different religions are all worshipping the same God, with different names, or do you think that each religion worships a different god? What evidence can you provide to support your view?

4 Sometimes religious people claim that there is only one way to God – and that is through following their particular religion. What would you say?

Arguments for the existence of God

On pages 86-89 of the textbook *Thinking Through Religion*, you can read about the **design argument** for the existence of God and the **argument from religious experience and revelation**. Here are some other arguments that are put forward for the existence of God, together with the objections that can be made against them.

The Cosmological Argument

"Cosmological" comes from the word "cosmos", meaning the universe. In the 13th century Thomas Aquinas argued that it is impossible for something to come from nothing. Therefore, the universe (the cosmos) must have been caused by something that existed before it. Aquinas argued that the first cause of everything must be eternal (without beginning or end). The first cause must be God.

In 1710 the philosopher Leibniz developed this argument by saying that nothing takes place without a "sufficient reason" – in other words, without a complete explanation. Leibniz said that, when we ask where the universe came from, we must find a complete explanation, which does not depend upon anything else. This will be God.

Objections

- You cannot move from saying that every event in the universe has a cause, to claiming that the universe itself has a cause. The philosopher Bertrand Russell (1872-1970) said that this is like moving from saying that each person has a mother, to claiming that the human race itself has a mother.
- If you argue that everything needs a complete explanation, what is your explanation for God? Where did God come from?
- Perhaps the universe itself is eternal, so it would not require anything to bring it into existence.

The Ontological Argument

The Ontological Argument was proposed by Saint Anselm in the 11th century. It starts by examining the definition of what God is for the religious believer. Anselm described God as "that than which nothing greater can be conceived". If God did not exist, something greater than Him could be conceived; therefore God must exist.

Objections

- Whatever a person can think of as existing – e.g. God – can also be thought of as not existing. The argument proves nothing.
- To say that God exists for the religious believer is not the same as saying that God exists as the creator of the universe. The Ontological Argument does not prove this. All it proves is that talk of God has meaning for the believer.

The Argument from Morality

All people have a sense of what is right and wrong. They have a conscience. Who gave them this conscience? This argument states that the conscience is a sign of God's existence. God gave people the ability to decide between good and evil. Some people (e.g. Mother Teresa) are inspired by their belief in God to behave completely selflessly.

Objections

- Some scientists argue that we learn our behaviour and our sense of right and wrong from our parents and our environment. It is these influences which condition us to behave as we do.
- There are many people who act selflessly who are not particularly religious (e.g. Diana, Princess of Wales).

WHAT TYPE OF GOD?

"If the Cosmological Argument succeeds, the uncaused cause, the unmoved mover, . . . is clearly going to be the . . . timeless God. This God is radically different from anything within the universe – nothing within the universe is the cause of itself and is dependent on nothing else . . . God is so transcendent and unknowable."

[Peter Vardy, *The Puzzle of God*, Fount, 1995]

Angels

"Angel" in Greek means "messenger". Angels are God's messengers in the world. They are spirit beings created by God. Islam teaches that angels have no free will.

1 In groups, share your ideas about angels. Do you think they exist? What do they look like? What is their purpose?

2 Read the story on this sheet about Winston Churchill, when he was British Prime Minister during the Second World War, and consider whether you think he may have come into contact with an angel on the occasion described.

3 Do you think that evidence of angels at work is proof of the existence of God? Provide reasons for your answer.

SOMETHING SAID TO ME "STOP!"

There was an occasion during the Blitz (bombing) when Churchill refused to ride in the armoured car provided for him, because it was so uncomfortable. Instead he commandeered a staff car. As he was about to get in,

"a strange thing occurred. The nearside door of the car was opened for him – he always sat on the nearside. For no apparent reason, he stopped, turned, opened the door on the other side of the car himself, got in, and sat there instead.

This was something he had never done before. On his way home, a bomb fell near the car, lifting it up on two wheels. If he had been sitting on the nearside, the car would have unquestionably turned over as the full force of the explosion lifted up the offside. Only Winston's extra weight had prevented disaster.

Although he didn't mention this escape to Clementine [his wife], she heard about it and asked, why did you get in on that side?

'I don't know, I don't know,' Winston answered at first. Then he said: 'Of course I know. Something said to me "Stop!" Before I reached the car door held open for me. It then appeared to me that I was told I was meant to open the door on the other side and get in and sit there.'"
[From *My Darling Clementine*, biography of Lady Churchill]

Religious Experience and Revelation

Think about your own life. Can you remember a time when you made a decision to change your attitudes, opinions, or actions (for example, when you stopped telling lies, or, even began to tell lies)?

Some people have dramatic religious experiences which cause them to change the way in which they live their life. Such experiences are sometimes called "peak experiences", because it seems that things come to a head; and then the person makes a conscious decision to change.

1 This sheet contains accounts of six religious experiences. As you read the accounts, consider what there is in common between the different experiences described. Also consider the effect that the experiences had on the people involved. Do such experiences prove that God exists?

(1) A white, bright, sparkling light

"I was 16 and had always enjoyed solitary walks around my village home. One evening I set out, by myself, as usual, to walk up a lane towards the wood. It must have been August . . . I was almost to the wood when I paused . . . Then . . . everything surrounding me was this white, bright, sparkling light, like sun on frosty snow, like a million diamonds, and there were no cornfields, no trees, no sky, this light was everywhere; my ordinary eyes were open but I was not seeing with them. It can only have lasted a moment I think or I would have fallen over. The feeling was indescribable, but I have never experienced anything in the years that followed that can compare with that glorious moment; it was blissful, uplifting, I felt open-mouthed wonder . . . We see God in the miracle of life, in trees, flowers and birds."

(2) An experience entirely out of time

"We came back from holiday to find that my mother had died unexpectedly and no one had been able to get in touch with us . . . At some point in the next few days – even before the funeral, I think – I had the most shattering experience of my entire life. I believe it was during a sleepless night, but it seems to have been an experience entirely out of time as we accept the notion. Without any sense perception I was made aware of a Reality beyond anything that my own mind could have conceived. And that Reality was a total love of all things in heaven and earth – For myself I have never doubted since that I was put in touch with that ultimate reality for which we use the shorthand 'God'."

(3) The most wonderful garden flowers

"After the sudden death of a four and a half year old son, I found no comfort in anything or anyone; the Church seemed powerless to help me, as did the medical profession. One morning I was dusting, tidying, the usual household chores, when I smelled the most wonderful garden flowers. It is difficult to describe the smell I mean – rather like a garden after rain. Being of a somewhat practical mind in such things, I looked around for the source of the smell. There were no flowers in the flat, certainly none outside, no perfumed polishes or toilet things in use. Then I sat down and for the first time since my son died I felt peaceful inside. I believe this was God's comfort; my son felt very near and I no longer felt alone. All I can tell you now is that I have no fear of what we call death. To me it will be shedding the material life for a spiritual life . . . "

(4) Forgiven and loved

"I can say that God is real to me. I know Him. I had a personal experience of the Lord Jesus Christ at my conversion at the age of 33. It was the most wonderful feeling of happiness I have ever known. I prayed to Jesus alone and it was after this, when lying in bed, I had this overwhelming feeling of happiness. It was all around my heart. I knew myself forgiven and loved."

Continued

(5) Healing

"My grandfather is a pastor and now and then I get the opportunity to travel with him. Last summer I went to Egypt with him. What I saw was amazing. We were in a small church just outside Cairo. At the end of the service my grandfather asked if anyone wanted to be prayed with – for healing. A lady in a wheelchair came forward. She had been crippled since her early twenties by a car accident. My grandfather laid hands on her and prayed for healing. Within minutes her legs started to move a little. My grandfather told her to stand. She looked at him and put her feet on the floor. She stood up. She explained that she felt a warm feeling flood through her. She could walk." [David, 16]

(6) A tremendous feeling of Divine Love

"I have had many beautiful experiences, but the most beautiful appears frequently. I can be driving in my car, walking down the street, working in my garden, etc. when all round me literally glows with light, colours become absolutely vibrant and such a tremendous feeling of Divine Love washes over me I feel attuned in perfect harmony with every living being in the universe. My life has been greatly changed. Animals come to me, people have written me and stopped me on lecture platforms and asked where the radiating light around me comes from. The only answer I can give is God. God is love, and if we become filled with true love for all things around us, we must radiate that love in our auras."

Note on sources

The account of "Healing" is from an interview with the author. All the other accounts on this sheet are from M. Maxwell and V. Tschudin, *Seeing the Invisible*, Arkana, 1990. Maxwell and Tschudin are researchers, who selected the accounts for their book from the Alistair Hardy Research Centre in Oxford.

Sample Examination Questions and Answers: The Existence of God

Total for questions [a], [b], and [c]: 20 marks

Read this newspaper cutting and answer questions [a], [b], and [c].

> **Majority of Britons "no longer believe in God"**
> by Steve Roth
>
> The majority of British people do not believe God exists, a new poll suggests. It is the first time a national survey has put believers in a minority.
>
> The MORI poll for the British Humanist Association, to be released next week, found that while 67 per cent of people consider themselves religious, only 43 per cent believe there is a God.
>
> [Source: S. Roth, *The Independent on Sunday*, 9 June 1996]

[a] According to this survey, 57 per cent of people in Britain do not believe in God. Give reasons why some people find it hard to believe in God today. [5 marks]

[b] If a group of religious people were to discuss their beliefs, what reasons might they give for believing in God? [10 marks]

[c] "If people live a good life and think of others, belief in God isn't really important." How far do you agree with this comment? Give reasons to support your answer and show that you have thought about different points of view. [5 marks]

Q [a] ANSWER ONE – GRADE A

Answer clearly focused on the question

Today technology and science can explain many things about the world and so <u>some people take the fact that no proof has been found for the existence of God to mean that God does not exist</u>. This argument is reinforced by the <u>apparent differences between what the sacred writings say about the origins of the universe and what scientists say</u>.

No proof for God's existence

Science/Religion debate

However, if there was proof that God existed, then there would be no need for faith, and without faith religion would be very different.

Today, with radio, television and the Internet, it is easier for people to find about all <u>the evil and suffering in the world</u>. When some people hear about so many man-made problems and natural disasters, they find it hard to believe in a God who is said to be <u>omnibenevolent, omniscient and omnipotent</u>. They think that God cannot be all of these things if evil and suffering exist, and if he is not all of these things then he is not God.

Good reference to problem of evil and suffering.

Good use of technical language

Q [a] ANSWER TWO – GRADE C

Lacks reference to evil and suffering, man-made problems, natural disasters

Today it is true that a lot of society does not believe in God. People say that they have to see to believe. <u>The Bible is evidence</u> that God does exist but how do we know whether this information is <u>reliable or not</u>?

Questions reliability of Bible

As times are changing, people are questioning God. The first question asked is who made God? And whoever made that person who made him? Today less pressure is put on people to believe in a certain religion. <u>A modern lifestyle may not have time for religion!</u>

Problems of being religious in a modern world

Many believers say that the design of the world is a reason to believe in God. This is known as the <u>Design Argument. It was suggested by William Paley</u>. The world is too complex to have been made by a coincidence. Then <u>the idea of evolution contradicts the design argument</u>. It can be said that belief in God begins here, as to whether you believe in the design argument or the idea of evolution.

Would be better placed in part [b]

Science/Religion debate

56

Clear and concise explanation of a whole range of ideas

Q [b] ANSWER ONE – GRADE A

Some people might give their own <u>religious experiences</u> as reasons for their belief in God. If they have felt moved by a feeling of divine presence in worship or when looking at the world, they might say that is evidence for the existence of God. Some people take faith healings and "miracles" to be proof of the existence of God. Some people may even have experienced a <u>"revelation" from God, such as the apparitions of the Virgin Mary or Saul</u> on the Damascus road. People's lives have been transformed by God.

Religious experiences explained

Revelation. Examples given.

Biblical evidence

 Some Christians say the <u>existence of the Bible</u> is their reason for belief in God. As it is God's word, that must prove that He exists. The fulfilment of the prophecies and similarities in the gospel accounts of the resurrection are evidence for the reality of the resurrection and therefore for the existence of God.

Idea of design

 Other people might use the <u>design argument</u> to show why they believe in God. They say that there is too much evidence of design and purpose in the universe for it to exist just by chance. There must be a designer and a maker – namely God.

Q [b] ANSWER TWO – GRADE C

If a group of religious people were to discuss their beliefs, they might say that the universe is too complex to just be a coincidence and an accident. <u>There is a purpose and a meaning to it just as there is a meaning and a purpose to a watch, as argued by William Paley.</u> Religious people may say that you may not believe because God has given you <u>free will</u> to believe in him or not. <u>The Bible is also evidence</u> that God existed. The early Christians witnessed Jesus, "the Messiah", come down from heaven to spread the word of the Lord and they recorded what Jesus did. The stories and fulfilment of the prophecies are too complicated to have just been made up. Some people also believe they have had <u>religious experiences</u> of God.

Several ideas which need developing for a higher grade.

Design argument

Perhaps more appropriate for Part [a]

Biblical evidence

Religious experience but no example

Good development of the statement under discussion

Q [c] ANSWER ONE – GRADE A

For some people living a good life, always thinking of others, is the most important thing. They think this is a good way to behave as it makes others happy and helps the less fortunate, but God isn't really considered. Some even point out the damage that religion can do – for instance, people are divided by their religions, as in the former Yugoslavia. It seems that religion doesn't help people to live in harmony. A humanist might take this view.

Christian viewpoint - recognises importance of both faith in God and living good life.

 However, for Christians, belief in God is very important. The Bible stresses the importance of having faith in God. In <u>John's Gospel, Jesus tells Nicodemus</u> that who believes in God's Son may not die but have eternal life. But the Bible also says it is important to live a good life. Jesus told a <u>story of the sheep and the goats, about the Last Judgement</u>. In this parable, people are judged according to how they have helped others, visited people in prison, fed the hungry, etc. Jesus told his disciples to love God but also to love your neighbour as yourself. He told the story of the <u>Good Samaritan</u> to show that loving your neighbour means loving everybody and helping them practically when they are in need.

Good Biblical evidence.

Balanced argument and opinions are supported with sound reasoning.

Good Biblical evidence.

Q [c] ANSWER TWO – GRADE C

We should all try to help those around us as we are part of the human race and so it is part of our duty. If people do live a good life and do think of others, then they are almost there to gain eternal life. But Jesus told us to <u>love our neighbour and believe in God</u>, not just one or the other. Some people may believe in God but still live an unhelpful and selfish life. So I think that it is ideal to make a useful contribution to the world and believe in God because then you are following the teachings of Christianity, to love God and other people.

Limited number of ideas which need developing.

Recognises that both ideas are important.

Suffering: What the Religions Say

BUDDHISM

The Four Noble Truths (see page 36 of the *Thinking Through Religion* student textbook) state that suffering (dukkha) is a part of life; that it has a cause; that it can be ended; and that the way to end suffering is to follow the Noble Eightfold Path.

"All that we are is the consequence of what we have thought." [Dhammapada]

"The world is afflicted with death and decay; therefore the wise do not grieve, knowing the terms of the world." [Buddhaghosa, "Voice of the Buddha", by a fifth-century Indian scholar]

CHRISTIANITY

"Come to me, all who labour and are heavy laden, and I will give you rest." [Matthew 11: 28]

"We rejoice in our sufferings, knowing that suffering produces endurance, and endurance produces character, and character produces hope, and hope does not disappoint us, because God's love has been poured into our hearts." [Romans 5: 3-5]

"It is better, if it is God's will, to suffer for doing good than for doing evil ..." [1 Peter 3: 17] and "rejoice that you participate in the sufferings of Christ, so that you may be overjoyed when his glory is revealed." [1 Peter 4: 13]

HINDUISM

"This body is mortal, always gripped by death, but within it dwells the immortal Self. This Self, when associated in our consciousness with the body, is subject to pleasure and pain; and so long as this association continues, freedom from pleasure and pain can no man find." [Chandogya Upanishad 8.12.1]

"The result of a virtuous action is pure joy; actions done out of passion bring pain and suffering." [Bhagavad Gita 14: 16]

ISLAM

"Be sure We shall test you with something of fear and hunger, some loss in goods or lives or the fruits of your toil, but give glad tidings to those who patiently persevere – who say when afflicted with calamity, 'To God we belong and to Him is our return'." [Qur'an, 2: 155-6]

"Secret counsels are only inspired by the Evil One, in order that he may cause grief to the believers; but he cannot harm them in the least, except as God permits; and in God let the believers put their trust." [Qur'an, 58: 10]

JUDAISM

"My son, do not despise the Lord's discipline ... for the Lord reproves him whom He loves, as a father the son in whom he delights." [Proverbs 3: 11-12]

"The Lord is my shepherd; I shall not want ... Yea, though I walk through the valley of the shadow of death, I will fear no evil; for Thou art with me; Thy rod and Thy staff they comfort me." [Psalm 23]

"He heals the broken-hearted, and binds up their wounds." [Psalm 147: 3]

SIKHISM

"Both poison and nectar are made by the Creator ... Everything is in the Creator's hands. We are given to eat as much of them as it pleases God to give us." [Guru Granth Sahib 1172-9]

1 What reasons for the existence of suffering are given in these quotations? Which do you agree with most? Explain why.

2 Can any good come out of suffering? What do the religions say about this?

3 Choose a quotation which helps you to understand suffering more. Explain why you chose it.

A Letter from God

This imaginary letter from God to Humanity is written from a Judaeo-Christian point of view.

Dearest Children,

I want to speak to you about suffering. Why does it even exist? It seems as though I am to blame for all the suffering in the world. You hold me responsible for inflicting pain on you. Well, I want you to know that nobody hates all this suffering more than I do. Although I might allow it, I do not inflict it on you. My love for you is a suffering love. It hurts me to see you in pain. Remember that I am always present on the side of those who suffer.

For you, suffering is a part of life. It is a necessary result of the gift of free will which I gave you when I created you. Much of the suffering which you live with is caused because you have made the wrong choices. You humans hurt each other with weapons of mass destruction, with your greed, and with your lack of compassion for your brothers and sisters who are in need. Your hatred, greediness, and jealousy have helped lead to countless wars and holocausts. You are responsible for spoiling the beautiful, harmonious world I intended you all to live in. The increasing pollution and damage to the environment are your doing.

There is a purpose in suffering. It is an important part of life. If there weren't any suffering, then you would all be stuck in a little plastic world. The challenges you face in suffering are the key to your spiritual and emotional growth. As one writer has put it: "pain is God's megaphone to rouse a deaf world . . . We think our childish toys bring us all the happiness that there is and our nursery is the whole wide world. But something must drive us out of the nursery to the world of others. And that something is suffering." Every suffering that you have to face is an experience from which you can learn. Suffering can be your teacher. Suffering can teach you patience and endurance and make you mature.

Suffering is a correction as well as a discipline, so do not despise the discipline of the Almighty. Do not consider suffering only as a judgement from me, but see it also as a purification process which results in you having a perfect relationship with me, your Maker. Take, for example, Job in the Bible. I allowed him to suffer terribly. However, even though everyone around him cursed my name and turned away from me, Job never turned away from me. To make gold and silver as pure as possible, they have to be put through the most intense fires. This is what I must do with you, my children. What kind of father would I be if I just let you have it your way all the time? How would you ever trust me or love me if I didn't discipline you for your wrongdoing?

I know some of this letter sounds harsh. I want you to know that I am your coach. I'll never push you further than you can go. Most importantly, you must know I am here for you. I have been with you all along and I will always be with you.

Finally, I would like to make it clear to you that my plans are not always understandable to you or accessible to human reasoning, in this world at least. Many things that seem incomprehensible to you now will only make better sense to you in eternal life. Instead of blaming me for the suffering in the world, I want you to run to me. If you ask, I will give you the strength to make it through.

Yours lovingly,

God.

Q

1 According to this letter, what is the cause of suffering? Do you agree?

2 According to this letter, what is the purpose of suffering? Do you agree?

3 Write your own letter in reply to this letter from God. Do you agree with all the sentiments in God's letter? What do you agree and disagree with? Give your reasons.

"God will save us"

Where is God when we suffer? The following story is one response to this question.

THE CART, THE BOAT, AND THE HELICOPTER

Once there was a terrible flood in a village and everybody fled for their lives – except for one family who stayed inside their house.

"Come on, get in!" called their friends in a cart, as the water started to cover the street.

"No, we'll stay here. God will save us."

"Hurry up! Climb aboard!" called other friends, sailing by in a boat, as the waters rose.

"No, we'll stay here," they replied from an upstairs window. "God will save us."

"Catch hold of this!" called some other friends, letting down a ladder from a helicopter.

"No, we'll stay here," they answered from the roof. "God will save us."

"How could you do this to us?" they accused God. "Why did you let us drown? Why didn't you save us?"

"I tried," God explained. "I sent the cart, the boat, and the helicopter!"

Q

1 In this story, what is the family's understanding of the statement that "God will save us"?

2 What is the story saying about what the statement means?

3 The story is a response to the question "Where is God when we suffer?" What do you think about the response it gives?

Sample Examination Questions and Answers: Suffering and Evil

Total for questions [a], [b], and [c]: 20 marks

[a] Explain, giving examples, the difference between suffering caused by evil human actions and suffering caused by nature. [5 marks]

[b] How are religious beliefs about suffering and evil linked to beliefs about what happens after death? [10 marks]

[c] "If there was no suffering in the world, there would be no need for religion!"
How far do you agree with this statement? Give reasons to support your answer and show that you have thought about different points of view. [5 marks]

---

shows clear understanding of the differences between evil human actions and suffering caused by nature.

Q [a] ANSWER ONE – GRADE A

Suffering can be caused by man and nature. Both types can be devastating, but one we can avoid. Natural suffering can be caused by such things as the weather and disease and is difficult to prevent.

Natural Suffering

Natural disasters, such as tornadoes, floods, avalanches, volcanic eruptions, earthquakes and typhoons, cause devastation around the world, killing thousands of people and leaving many people homeless. These disasters cannot be prevented by humankind. Some Christians believe that diseases and natural disasters are the result of the Fall (original sin). Natural suffering doesn't seem as sinister as suffering caused by evil human actions.

Good examples.

Biblical reference to the Fall.

Evil Human Actions

Good examples.

One example of suffering caused by evil human actions is the Holocaust in Nazi Germany, when millions of Jews were brutally gassed. Another example could be the Dunblane massacre, where a maniac killed some innocent children for no apparent reason. These kinds of event happen because humans have free will, given to us by God, and choose to do terrible things.

Good reference to free will.

Clearly defines both evil human actions and suffering caused by nature.

Q [a] ANSWER TWO – GRADE C

The suffering humans create is caused by our free will given by God. We create our own suffering and evil by doing evil actions such as rape, murder and war. Natural disasters are different because they are out of our control and are the result of events which happen naturally. They include things like earthquakes, floods, hurricanes and volcanic eruptions. They can cause much devastation and loss of human life.

Reference to free will.

Shows understanding.

Good examples.

Link between our actions and our destiny in the next life.

Q [b] ANSWER ONE – GRADE A

Muslims believe in the mercy of Allah but they also believe that evil actions will be punished in the afterlife. A person who ignores Allah and is selfish and fails to live in obedience to Islam is in great danger of ending up in jahannam (hell). According to the Qur'an, this is a place of torment, of great heat and black smoke. Those who moan and groan against Allah when times of suffering come will also face punishment on the Day of Judgement, because Allah may well have sent the difficulties in order to test them. Allah is Omnipotent and Omniscient, and so Muslims believe that suffering is for a purpose. Muslims are encouraged to endure suffering without complaint and avoid doing evil deeds.

Correct use of technical language.

Description of Jahannam.

Idea of testing.

Idea of heaven.

Muslims believe that those who do good and obediently follow Allah will have the reward in the afterlife of going to paradise. So how you react to suffering and evil affects your destiny. If you do evil, then Muslims believe that you will fall off the Assirat bridge into eternal torment and not be able to cross into the beautiful paradise (heaven) as it is described in the Qur'an.

Idea of judgement.

Q [b] ANSWER TWO – GRADE C

Salvation through Jesus.

Catholic belief.

Reference to Purgatory (technical term.)

Christians believe that sin causes suffering and entered the world at the Fall. God is holy and does not like evil but sent Jesus to die in our place, so that we can be forgiven. So the belief you have in God affects where you go when you die. If you believe and trust in Jesus as your saviour then your spirit will go to Heaven and God. If you don't believe, then on the Day of Judgement you will be judged for the evil you have done and be banished to spend eternity in Hell.

Roman Catholics believe (particularly in the Middle Ages) that if you have believed in God but committed many sins and not repented, then your spirit will go to Purgatory. Here your spirit is cleansed of sins and then can proceed to Heaven.

Reference to the Fall and to belief in forgiveness through Jesus.

Idea of Judgement.

Q [c] ANSWER ONE – GRADE A

Answer clearly focused on suffering and the importance of religion.

Most Christians believe that the Bible and Christianity hold the answers to much more than just suffering. Because of the Resurrection of Jesus, Christians look forward to their next life with God in heaven. In that case, religion can be seen to be very important, even if there was no suffering. Religion also guides us how to live and act with love towards our neighbours. There would be a need for this guidance even if there wasn't suffering in the world. People also believe in a supernatural being who created the universe and there would be a vacuum in many people's lives if they did not have someone to worship.

Reference to Resurrection and life after death.

Need for guidance.

Idea of worship.

Religion helps those who suffer.

Shows the importance of the Bible for a clear understanding of why Jesus died.

Others, however, may believe in meditation or yoga or other spiritual experiences without a formal belief in God as an answer to suffering. Without suffering they may not feel the same need for religion and prayer. In many instances religion may be an answer to help people get through suffering and therefore not so vitally important if suffering ceased.

On the other hand, the Bible is a constant reminder of how Jesus suffered on the cross and died to save us from our sins, so Christians would be reminded of suffering when reading the Bible. In conclusion, I would say that if there was no suffering in the world, Christians would believe that that is because God is Omnipotent and therefore prevents His human race from suffering. So it would still be important to worship God.

Alternative view.

Gives personal opinion with argument.

Use of technical language.

Q [c] ANSWER TWO – GRADE C

Appropriate examples to support opinion.

I do not totally agree because, for religious people, their belief is not just for the bad times when they need help, but also for the good times. Religion is there when you are down, and when suffering is occurring. However it also is there for weddings, christenings, Bar Mitzvahs and other religious celebrations. Religion is not seen as an easy way out of suffering because, for most people, religion is a way of life and is of deep spiritual meaning in their life.

Recognises the need for religion.

Sound reasoning.

Alternative viewpoint.

However, if there was no suffering in the world, then people wouldn't feel the need to pray for help to a "good" God or ask for forgiveness of our sins. If there was not suffering, people would probably forget about God and His good works because people wouldn't realise how "well off" their situation is.

Additional reason.

Personal viewpoint.

Therefore I think, if there was no suffering, then people may begin to forget about religion and God, but a large majority would still need it.

Is there a life after death?: What the Religions Say

BUDDHISM

"Not in the sky, nor deep in the ocean, nor in a mountain cave is there a spot in the world where, if a man abide there, death could not overtake him." [Dhammapada 128]

"The body dies but the spirit is not entombed." [Dhammapada 151]

"When a man considers this world as a bubble of froth, and as the illusion of an appearance, then the king of death has no power over him . . . This world is indeed darkness, and how few can see the light! Just as few birds escape from the net, so few souls can fly into the freedom of heaven." [Dhammapada 170, 174]

CHRISTIANITY

"Do not lay up for yourselves treasures on earth, where moth and rust consume and where thieves break in and steal, but lay up for yourselves treasure in heaven, where neither moth nor rust consumes and where thieves do not break in and steal. For where your treasure is, there will your heart be also." [Matthew 6: 19-21]

"In my Father's house are many rooms." [John 14: 2]

"I saw the dead, great and small, standing before the throne and books were opened . . . The dead were judged according to what they had done as recorded in the books." [Revelation 20: 11-12]

HINDUISM

"As a man passes from dream to wakefulness, so does he pass from this life to the next." [Brihadaranyaka Upanishad 4.3.35]

"As a man casts off his worn-out clothes and takes on other new ones in their place, so does the embodied soul cast off his worn-out bodies and enters others anew . . . For sure is the death of all that comes to birth, sure the birth of all that dies." [Bhagavad Gita 2: 22,27]

"From the unreal lead me to the real, from darkness lead me to light, from death lead me to immortality." [Brihadaranyaka Upanishad 1.3.28]

ISLAM

"You prefer this life, although the life to come is better and more enduring." [Qur'an, 87: 16-17]

"[On the Day of Judgement] shall all men be sorted out. Then those who have believed and worked righteous deeds shall be made happy in a mead of delight. And those who have rejected faith and falsely denied Our signs and the meeting of the Hereafter – such shall be brought forth to punishment." [Qur'an, 30: 14-16]

"The ones who disbelieve will be driven along to hell in throngs . . . What an awful lodging it will be . . . The ones who have heeded their Lord will be driven along to the Garden." [Qur'an, 39]

JUDAISM

"This world is like an antechamber to the world to come; prepare thyself in the antechamber that thou mayest enter into the hall." [Mishnah]

"Not like this world is the World to Come. In the World to Come there is neither eating nor drinking; no procreation of children or business transactions; no envy or hatred or rivalry; but the righteous sit enthroned, their crowns on their heads, and enjoy the lustre of the Divine Splendour." [Talmud]

SIKHISM

"After you depart this life, God shall demand a reckoning of your deeds that in his ledger are recorded. Those that are rebellious shall be summoned . . . the angel of death will hover over them, and trapped in a blind alley they will not know any escape. Says Nanak, any falsehood must be destroyed. Truth in the end shall prevail." [Guru Granth Sahib]

1 List the images used in these quotations to describe (a) the passage from this life to the next, (b) the next life.

2 What ideas about life after death do the religions share? How do the religions differ in their ideas about the subject?

Attitudes to Death

Today approximately 200,000 people died. Their deaths were caused by accident, murder, alcohol, starvation ... Some died while still in the womb. Others died of old age. Death is the one certainty of life. This activity sheet looks at different reactions that people have to death – some fight death, others accept it peacefully.

The attitude many of us have towards our inevitable death is illustrated in the story of the Edinburgh Train.

> "Every man knows that he must die, but no one believes it."
> [Yiddish Proverb]

> "Dying is an art. I do it exceptionally well."
> [Sylvia Plath]

THE EDINBURGH TRAIN

Suppose you're using the train from London to Edinburgh. You get on the train and think: This is very nice: I think I'll stay here forever! You put your name over the carriage, put curtains up in your compartment, and decide you have "Quite a nice little home".

Then you reach Edinburgh and the porter comes on and tells you to leave the train. But you're clinging to the seat saying, "I don't want to get off! This compartment's so nice!" The porter explains that it's in the nature of trains that you get off them at the end of the line. In reply you cry out, "But I refuse to accept that!"

There has to be a mature way of dealing with this: a painless way of getting off a train! But how do you do that? Well, the easiest way is to acknowledge, when you get on the train, that you will have to get off again, and not get too comfortable.

It's the same when you find yourself inhabiting your body, your life situation. From the very beginning, acknowledge that you will have to get off again at some point. Whilst I'm here, for sure, I can enjoy this carriage, this body, but I must not cling too tightly, because one day I will have to give it up.

1 Although we all die, and we all know we are going to die, most of us avoid talking about death. It is a "taboo" subject (i.e. there seems to be a kind of rule that it should not be spoken about). Why do you think this is? Do you ever talk about death? Have you ever come close to death? Have you ever seen a dead body?

2 Sometimes we even hide from using the actual word "die". Instead, we use other expressions such as "kick the bucket"/fall asleep/pass away. What other words and phrases do people use for "die", "dead", and "death"? Have you heard any? Why do you think people avoid using "die", "dead", and "death"?

3 In the story of the Edinburgh Train, what do you think of the passenger's reaction to being on the train? What do you think this story is trying to teach us about life and death? Does the story correctly describe our attitude to death? Do you think it is possible to "enjoy this carriage" (i.e. enjoy living) without clinging on to life itself?

Continued

4　Thinking about death can be a religious experience, as the following accounts show. Use these accounts to write a paragraph explaining the importance of death for helping us to live well.

Death gives loveliness to life

There is a story of a teacher who was about to die. His disciples became depressed.

"Don't you see that death gives loveliness to life?" said the teacher.

"No, we'd much rather you never died," said one disciple.

"Whatever is truly alive must die," said the teacher. "Look at the flowers: only plastic flowers never die."

[adapted from Anthony de Mello, *One Minute Wisdom*, Doubleday, 1983]

A new sense of priorities

Robert Wilkins wrote this less than a year after being told that he had cancer:

"At present the growths on my liver are contained and apparently inactive. Meanwhile, life has taken on a new vividness and sense of urgency. One ensures that time is put to the fullest possible use. There is a new sense of priorities. Relationships are fully valued, and extremely rewarding. I really want to know how this friend is faring, what problems and satisfactions he or she is encountering. Each day is used to greatest advantage, as carpe diem – seize the day – has become my motto."

[Taken from *Oxford Friends Meeting Newsletter*, October 1990]

A healing of my spirit

"I don't expect to be cured. Now that doesn't mean I don't *want* to be cured or *hope* to be cured. I am always hoping that there is some miracle drug right around the corner. But now I feel like this: it's OK to die of AIDS and it's OK to be cured of AIDS. I realize that some things have happened within me that could not have happened if I had been physically well. I mean things like a healing of my spirit, an acceptance of myself, an opening to God. So in a way, I am healed even when my T-cells are down. I would not trade this feeling for anything in the world."

[quoted in Debra Jarvis, *HIV Positive*, Lion Publishers]

If . . .

"When the Ben-Yehuda bombings [in Jerusalem, Israel, in 1997] took place in Jerusalem I was only a few metres away from the explosion. If I had not stayed that extra five minutes at school, I may not be here now. It taught me to be fearful of death, knowing that it could happen at any time."

[Kalle, aged 18]

5　If you knew you were going to die in the very near future, to whom would you write "thank you" letters? What would you say in these letters? Choose one person and write out the letter. Why wait until your death to give it to them?

Reincarnation Row

Hoddle sacked for slur on disabled

[3 February 1999]

GLENN HODDLE, England's football coach, was sacked yesterday. The Football Association explained that they had had to sack him because he had damaged himself and the FA, as his employers, by his remarks in an interview with *The Times* in January.

Hoddle has spoken before about his own particular belief in reincarnation. In last month's newspaper interview he suggested that disabled people were paying for their sins in a previous life.

At a press conference after his sacking, Hoddle, wearing a pale grey check suit, said that he had "made an error of judgement" and that it had never been his intention to cause offence.

Many groups representing disabled people welcomed Hoddle's departure. Mencap commented that: "It is only right that the English coach pays a just penalty for comments which caused a great offence and fuelled more bigotry towards those who already face prejudice."

Hindus, who traditionally believe in reincarnation, have pointed out that there is a difference between their beliefs and Hoddle's. Hindu belief is that what people sow they will reap, but Hindus are taught not to be judgemental and to treat all people as equals. They have criticised Hoddle for making judgements about disabled people and underlined the Hindu teaching of compassion and care for all. A Hindu priest from London also explained: "Those who are less fortunate understand the reasons for their circumstances and it is through this understanding that their faith in God is enhanced."

What Hoddle said on radio

"I have got an inner belief and an inner faith with God. I do believe spiritually we have to progress because we've been here before. The physical body is just an overcoat for your spirit. At death you take the overcoat off and your spirit will go on to another life in a spirit dimension. I think we make mistakes when we are down here and our spirit has to come back and learn. That's why there is an injustice in the world. Why there's certain people born into the world with terrible physical problems and why there's a family who has got everything right, physically and mentally."

[Interview on BBC Radio Five, 17 May `17 1998]

1 Why was Glenn Hoddle sacked? Do you think it was right that he was sacked?

2 Compare Hoddle's comments with Hindu beliefs about reincarnation. In what ways are they the same? How do they differ?

3 Why do you think some people believe that public figures like Glenn. Hoddle should keep their religious views private? Do you think they should?

Sample Examination Questions and Answers: Life after Death

Total for questions [a], [b], and [c]: 20 marks

[a] Explain what life after death will be like according to the religious beliefs you have studied. [8 marks]

[b] Explain how religious beliefs about life after death may affect a person's behaviour in this life. [7 marks]

[c] "There is no evidence for survival after death." How far do you agree with this statement? Give reasons to support your answer and show that you have thought about different points of view. [5 marks]

Shows clear understanding of the Day of Judgement and need to earn place in heaven.

Shows understanding of difficulty of explaining something unparalleled in human experience.

Q [a] ANSWER ONE – GRADE A

People who follow Islam believe in a Day of Reckoning when they will have to give an account of their actions during their life on earth. They believe that the way a person lives on earth determines whether he or she earns a place in heaven.

According to Islam, when you die, the angel of death takes your soul to barzakh. This is a state of waiting between the moment of death and the Day of Judgement. After judgement you will enter either paradise or hell (jahannam). The Qur'an describes a state of joy, peace and beauty which is the reward for leading a good, believing life. Paradise is described as being like a beautiful green garden full of flowers and the songs of birds. "A cup will be passed to them from a clear-flowing fountain – which is delicious to drink." Muslims say it is difficult to find appropriate language to really describe Paradise, because it is a place of unimaginable delight and reward for faithful believers.

Hell is described as a horrible place full of fire, hot winds, black smoke and boiling water. It is a place where people will be tortured and tormented for living selfish lives. Some of the language used to describe hell may be symbolic but it is clear that Muslims believe that it is a place to be avoided.

Good use, and explanation, of technical language.

Description supported by evidence from the Qur'an.

Good summary.

Understands that language may be symbolic.

Q [a] ANSWER TWO – GRADE C

Includes belief in afterlife in heaven or hell.

Differences in belief.

Christians believe that, because of the resurrection of Jesus, they too will have eternal life. Many Christians believe that the afterlife will be either in heaven or hell. In the Middle Ages hell was often pictured as a place of eternal torture for sinners. Heaven is described in the Bible as a place of sheer delight, living in the presence of God for ever. Particularly years ago, Roman Catholics believed in purgatory, which was like a half-way house where a person went to be cleansed before going to heaven. Protestants believe that sins are forgiven through Jesus and that souls go immediately to be with God in heaven.

Descriptions of hell and heaven.

Reference to Purgatory.

Lacks Biblical quotes. No mention of symbolic language.

Q [b] ANSWER ONE – GRADE A

Muslims believe that Allah tests our characters by testing our reactions to both good fortune and misfortune to see if we are full of complaint or arrogant or unforgiving. Muslims try to avoid these things and live a life considering others and helping those in need. In Islam, angels are believed to keep a full record of each person's actions, throughout life. Muslims try to behave in such a way that they earn a place in heaven (Paradise).

According to Islam, it is too late to ask Allah's forgiveness when you die. You must behave well in this life in order to earn the reward of Paradise. This idea spurs Muslims on to keep the practices of praying five times a day and fasting during

Idea that life is a test.

Salvation can be earned.

Link between belief and practice

Correct use of several technical terms.

daylight hours during the month of <u>Ramadan</u>. The temptation to cheat must be great, but they believe their guardian angels will know if they do. The belief that they must earn their place in Paradise also encourages them to live modestly and give to charity (<u>Zakah</u>).

Diversity within the religion.

There are <u>differences within Islam</u>, with the fundamentalists demanding a much more strict lifestyle: e.g. women should not work and should cover all of their bodies apart from their hands and face.

It appears that fear of going to hell (<u>jahannam</u>) is very real although Muslims would probably say that they live as they do because of their love for Allah and the encouragement of reward in Paradise.

No analysis of the relative importance of faith and works. No diversity within Christianity.

Q [b] ANSWER TWO – GRADE C

Christians believe that it is important to live good helpful lives in order to go to heaven and avoid hell. Also, they try to live good lives to set an example as followers of Jesus. Christians do in general <u>follow the teachings of Jesus and pray, fast and give to people in need (the duties as described in the Sermon on the Mount)</u>. They try to live lives which are devoted to Jesus, not so much in fear of the afterlife but rather because they believe it is right to <u>respond to the love of God</u>. Christians also believe that it depends on our beliefs as to whether we go to heaven. So <u>both belief and asking God to forgive them for their sin are important</u>.

Reference to following Jesus's teaching in the Sermon on the Mount.

Response to God's love.

Importance of beliefs and asking for forgiveness.

Reference to holy writings.

Q [c] ANSWER ONE – GRADE A

Muslims and Christians would say that there is life after death because <u>both the Qur'an and the Bible</u> say that there is. Christians point to the <u>resurrection of Jesus</u> and say that if there is no such thing as survival after death, then Jesus Christ could not have come back to life. Does this prove that there is something in it? Not necessarily. But there are people who claim to have had <u>near-death experiences</u>, and these are another thing which suggests that there is life after death.

Discussion of resurrection of Jesus.

secular idea of proof.

Idea of faith, which could have been developed.

Perhaps near-death experiences are hoaxes, by people who wish to become famous. Or the experiences could be encoded in the brain to ease the pain of death. How do we know if these are genuine experiences? Even the resurrection of Jesus could have been a hoax. <u>Did the writers tell the truth?</u> Did Jesus really die on the cross and rise again? Did he just faint or go into a coma? Was he rescued from the tomb by his followers? Did they steal the body? These are many questions for which I do not definitely know the answer. In the end it seems to me to come down to <u>a matter of faith and belief</u> which millions of people do possess.

Discusses reliability of evidence.

Other ideas and reasons.

Q [c] ANSWER TWO – GRADE C

<u>Evidence from tombs in ancient Egypt and China</u> shows that belief in an afterlife has been around for thousands of years. In recent times people have claimed to have had <u>near-death experiences</u> – for example, out-of-body experiences where seriously ill patients peer down from above their own body in hospital. Some claim to have been drawn along a long tunnel towards a bright light.

Evidence from ancient civilisations.

Reasons why these beliefs may or may not be true.

These could all be hoaxes by people who wish to become famous. <u>We haven't really got any proof</u> that they are telling the truth. It might be that they are deliberately lying or that lack of oxygen to the brain has caused delusions.

Reference to faith and the Resurrection.

To me it seems to be <u>a matter of faith, just like Christians believing in the Resurrection of Jesus</u>. We will probably never know the answer until we die ourselves.

Lacks emphasis on religious ideas/evidence.

Life and Death Issues

Chapters 10-12 of *Thinking Through Religion* cover some of the most challenging debates facing contemporary society. They are also perennial debates. As teachers and GCSE examiners, we add a caution: often students become so involved in the pros and cons of each debate that they overlook key issues and the application of religious principles and sacred texts. This course attempts to avoid this problem by engaging students in a cross-examination of the religious teachings as they apply to the issues. The chapters address the following topics:

Is abortion right or wrong?

▹ The sanctity of life as it relates to the issues surrounding abortion
▹ The concepts of the quality of life and the nature of life as a gift
▹ The rights of those involved
▹ Contemporary debate (social and cultural context of the debate) and legislation in Great Britain
▹ Religious and non-religious arguments about abortion

Should euthanasia be allowed?

▹ Key concepts, including the sanctity of life, quality of life, when does human life end?
▹ The rights of those involved. What does it mean to say "people have a right to live"?
▹ Contemporary debate (social and cultural context of the debate) and legislation in Great Britain

▹ The different forms of euthanasia (e.g. voluntary, passive)
▹ Religious and non-religious arguments about euthanasia

Is it ever right to go to war?

▹ The issues which divide human beings and cause conflict
▹ Different forms of conflict (e.g. aggressive, defensive); killing in peace time and killing in war
▹ The nature of peace
▹ Concepts such as Just War and Holy War and their application to modern-day war
▹ Religious responses to war and peace (e.g. non-violent resistance, pacifism)

Examination candidates will be expected to:

▹ be aware of relevant religious teachings from sacred texts, religious principles, and contemporary religious leaders and organisations;
▹ demonstrate knowledge and understanding of the diversity of viewpoints held by believers within a single religious tradition;
▹ develop the ability to make reasoned and informed judgements about religious and, where appropriate, other responses to ethical issues.

Activity Sheet/Study Skills Sheet	Key concept for students to consider
B.1 Cloning	Is genetic engineering ethical? Do people have a right to play God?
10.1 Abortion: What the Religions Say	Quotations from six world religions.
10.2 Anna's Story	Rights and responsibilities in the case of abortion.
10.3 Classrooms of Boys	Report from China, giving different perspective on abortion.
11.1 Euthanasia: What the Religions Say	Quotations from five world religions.
11.2 Euthanasia: Patient and Doctor Speak Out	Arguments for and against euthanasia.
11.3 Exam Questions and Answers*	Sample questions and graded answers on Euthanasia.
12.1 War and Peace: What the Religions Say	Quotations from six world religions.
12.2 With God on our side!	Why people fight in the name of religion.
12.3 The madness of war	Non-violent protest against war.
12.4 Exam Questions and Answers*	Sample questions and graded answers on War and Peace.

* *See Grade Descriptions on page 124.*

Cloning

Government creates a panel on bio-ethics

[3 February 1999]

The Government has set up a panel to discuss bio-ethics. It has noted concerns amongst young people about cloning, genetically modified food, and gene research.

Scientists have discovered so much about genes, and about DNA (the chemical that genes are made of), that they can manipulate the make-up of living things. For example, they can alter the genetic make-up of a fruit so that it will ripen more slowly than it does naturally. It is also possible to produce exact copies of living things, using material in their cells. These exact copies are called clones.

In 1997, the first ever clone of an adult animal was produced: a sheep called Dolly. She was made by taking a single cell from an adult sheep and putting its genetic material into an egg cell which had been stripped of its own DNA. The egg cell was placed inside a female sheep, who eventually gave birth to Dolly. Dolly was an exact copy of the sheep from which the original cell was taken. There is great debate about whether cloning humans would be wrong or right. On the one hand it offers the possibility of avoiding hereditary illnesses (conditions passed on genetically from a parent to a child). It would also be an answer for couples who are infertile. On the other hand, some people think that cloning threatens the uniqueness of each human life.

Ann McElvoy, writing in *The Independent* newspaper, commented:

"At present, genetics sounds scary because the only accessible image we have of it in practice is Dolly the sheep. That will change once the benefits of tissue-cloning are seen in the bypassing of hereditary diseases and the replacement of missing limbs. The 'Frankenstein doctors' who are 'playing God' in the headlines today will become the 'miracle-workers' of tomorrow ... [However] the divide between cloning tissue and cloning people, which the regulatory bodies are now seeking to keep intact, will soon prove porous."

1 Ann McElvoy refers to a difference between cloning human tissue and cloning people. Can you explain what this difference is? What point is Ann McElvoy making about the difference?

2 What do you think are the potential dangers of human cloning?

3 Is human cloning a matter of "playing God"? Would it threaten the uniqueness of each human being?

Abortion: What the Religions Say

This page presents quotations from various religious sources. It is important that you use this sheet together with pages 118-122 of the *Thinking Through Religion* student textbook, to see how the religions have applied these passages to the subject of abortion.

Q

1 What beliefs about the sanctity of life do the religions share?

2 Make a list of reasons given by the religions against allowing abortion. Which reason do you agree with most? Write a sentence explaining why.

BUDDHISM

"Being reborn as a human is as likely as a blind turtle which is swimming in a large ocean and surfaces once every one hundred years, putting its head through a small golden ring which is floating on the surface of the water." [Tibetan Buddhism]

"We consider abortion to be the same as taking the life of a living being and as such as not a just action. However, there can be exceptional circumstances . . . where it is certain that the child will be born with abnormalities or where the mother's life is in danger."[Dalai Lama, *Beyond Dogma: the challenge of the modern world*, Souvenir Press, 1994]

CHRISTIANITY

"Human life must be respected and protected absolutely from the moment of conception." [Catechism of the Catholic Church]

"We . . . believe that abortion is an evil . . . But we also believe that to withdraw compassion is evil . . . Christians need to face frankly the fact that in an imperfect world the 'right' choice is sometimes the lesser of two evils." [General Synod of the Church of England]

HINDUISM

"His being is the source of all being . . . He is God, hidden in all beings, their inmost soul who is in all. He watches the works of creation, lives in all things, watches all things." [Svetasvatara Upanishad]

"Unborn, eternal, everlasting he [the soul] is primeval: he is not slain when the body is slain. If a man knows him as indestructible, eternal, unborn, never to pass away, how and whom can he cause to be slain or slay?" [Bhagavad Gita]

ISLAM

"Kill not your children on a plea of want." [Qur'an, 6: 151]

"Do not kill your children in fear of poverty. We shall provide for both them and you. Killing them is a big sin." [Quran, 17: 31]

"No severer of womb relationship ties will ever enter paradise." [Hadith]

"Allah fixes the time span for all things . . . it is He who causes people to die and to be born." [Qur'an, 53: 42-47]

JUDAISM

"See now that I myself am He! There is no god beside me. I put to death and I bring to life." [Deuteronomy 32: 39]

"You shall not murder." [Exodus 20: 13]

"Before I formed you in the womb I knew you, before you were born I set you apart." [Jeremiah 1: 5]

"You created every part of me; You put me together in my mother's womb." [Psalm 139: 13]

"If a woman in labour has a life-threatening difficulty, one dismembers the embryo within her, removing it limb by limb, for her life takes precedence over its life. But once its greater part has emerged it may not be harmed, for we do not set aside one life for another." [Talmud]

SIKHISM

"Abortion is morally wrong as it is interference in the creative work of God." [From an article by Mansukhani in *The Sikh Messenger*]

Anna's Story

Anna is 18 years old and has been with her boyfriend, Sami, for just over a year. To celebrate the end of their A-levels Anna and Sami joined their friends for a party. They both had too much to drink and as the evening developed they ended up in bed together. They had never gone this far together before, and failed to use any contraceptives.

It is now a few weeks later and Anna is worried that she has not had her period. She uses a home pregnancy testing kit. What she feared is true – she is pregnant. Her hopes of a bright university career are shattered. She loves Sami but had not seen herself settling down with him, at least not for the next few years. Moreover, how is she going to tell her religious parents? They have strong views on abortion.

Anna feels isolated and confused. She turns to you for help and advice.

As you answer these questions you can choose which religion Anna's parents belong to.

1 What are the choices Anna has to make?

2 What might the following people be thinking: Sami, Anna's parents, Anna herself?

3 Does Sami have any rights in this case?

4 Should anyone else be involved in the decision?

5 If Anna goes ahead with the pregnancy, what might life be like?

6 Who should make the final decision? Should religious principles affect any decision that is to be made? Explain why.

7 What advice would you give Anna?

Classrooms of Boys

A newspaper article in 1999 included photographs from China: one showed a primary school classroom with boys out-numbering girls by about 12 to 1; another showed an abandoned baby girl lying in the street. The article explained that there was something "odd, and more than a little sinister about these serried ranks of eager, happy, healthy little Chinese boys".

"For two decades now, China, with a population of 1.3 billion, has operated a draconian 'one-child-one family' policy. In theory, a good idea: China has around one-quarter of the world's population, but only 7 per cent of the world's arable land. If the population grows too fast, then starvation might well result . . .

The fine for a second child in the city (rural families are allowed two if the first is a girl) is now £9,000 – a fortune when the average rural wage is less than £30 a month.

'The pressure for a boy is too much,' [said one mother]. 'Most of my friends pay a doctor for a scan [this is illegal] . . . often they will stay with the doctor for an illegal abortion.'

Ninety-seven per cent of all abortions (many of them brutally enforced by the dreaded Birth Control Committees to prevent the 'unauthorised' birth of an extra child) are estimated to be of female babies.

When it comes to punishing those who break the 'one-child' rule, the Birth Control Committees appear to have untrammelled powers."

[from an article by Ann Leslie in the *Daily Mail*, 3 July 1999]

1 Why does China have such a high abortion rate?

2 Do you think abortion should be available for such political and economic reasons?

3 Does a country have a right to dictate how many children a couple can have?

Euthanasia: What the Religions Say

This page presents quotes from various religious sources. It is important that you use this sheet together with pages 127-131 of the *Thinking Through Religion* student textbook to see how the religions have applied these passages to the issue of euthanasia.

1 Make a list of the reasons why the religions are against euthanasia. Do the religions have beliefs in common?

BUDDHISM

"It is a delicate problem, one that cannot be answered on the basis of general suggestions. Above all, one must consider the motivation behind the act." [Dalai Lama, *Beyond Dogma: the challenge of the modern world*, Souvenir Press, 1994]

CHRISTIANITY

"You are God's temple and God's Spirit lives in you! So if anyone destroys God's temple, God will destroy him. For God's temple is holy, and you yourselves are his temple." [1 Corinthians 3: 16-17]

HINDUISM

"Non-violence is the highest ethical code of behaviour. It includes non-killing, non-injury and non-harming. Do not kill any living creature . . . Do not kill a human being . . . Do not commit suicide." [Shikshapatri of Swaminarayan]

ISLAM

"Nor can a soul die except by God's leave, the term being fixed as by writing." [Qur'an, 3: 145]

"O ye who believe . . . do not kill yourselves: for verily God hath been to you most merciful." [Qur'an, 4: 29]

"The Prophet said, 'In the time before you, a man was wounded. His wounds troubled him so much that he took a knife and cut his wrist to bleed himself to death. Thereupon Allah said, "My slave hurried in the matter of his life; therefore he is deprived of the Garden".'" [Hadith]

JUDAISM

"The Lord has given, and the Lord has taken away." [Job 1: 21]

Euthanasia: Patient and Doctor Speak Out

1 Read through the two accounts on this sheet. Collect reasons for and against euthanasia.

2 Do you think the chronically ill man has a right to sign a "living will"?

MY LIFE IS SO LONELY – A CHRONICALLY ILL MAN

Peter Raynor, 61, is managing director of his own travel firm in Wetherby, Yorkshire. He was diagnosed as having Multiple Sclerosis 26 years ago. Recently he consulted lawyers to draw up an advance directive, or "living will". He says:

"The times when I enjoyed life are long gone. I am partially sighted, doubly incontinent and I cannot wash, dress or feed myself. I haven't stood up alone since 1981, can't turn over in bed and I am seldom free from pain. If I were a dog or cat, I would have been put down long ago.

"I have contemplated suicide many times, but it is not a matter of choice, it is simply a question of ability. And even if someone offered to help me, I would have to refuse. I would be implicating them in a criminal offence.

"I know my chances of remission at this stage of the disease are extremely remote and I am still deteriorating. That is why, last year, I signed an advance directive. It states that, in specific circumstances listed in the document, I do not wish to be kept alive by medical technology. The document has no legal status, but my doctor and solicitor have copies, so at least there is written proof of my wishes, should the time come when I am unable to express them.

"I get so angry with these pro-Life people. I would like to take one person from that movement, and sit them in my wheelchair, blindfolded, their hands tied, and refuse them the chance to go to the toilet. A few weeks of that and I feel sure they would no longer speak with the same conviction."

Continued

HIS PAIN WAS TOO MUCH FOR HIM TO BEAR – DR STEPHEN HENDERSON SMITH

"A doctor's job is to relieve suffering. Why should one allow nature to take its long and painful course when you have the means to help people immediately?

"One of my first patients, an elderly man, had pneumonia which, in 1942 when the supply of antibiotics was inadequate and penicillin wasn't available, was considered a terminal illness. He begged me to help him die. His pain was too much for him to bear. I struggled for days with my conscience and, eventually, I gave him a dose of morphine that was just over the usual limit. I remember thinking, if death occurs, so be it. I wanted to release him.

"Ten years ago a man I had never seen before came into my surgery just as I was about to leave and asked to be seen as a private patient. He was in his late seventies and had bronchitis and emphysema. Every breath he took was agony. He told me that he wanted to end his life.

"I said that I couldn't risk the legal complication, but he was so desirous of a way out of his pain and suffering that he begged me, 'If you can't do it, at least tell me how many of my tablets I should take to be sure of death'. I wrote '30' on a piece of paper.

"The following week I read in the local paper that he had died. For some time I felt very nervous that I would be arrested. People knew my views on euthanasia. A doctor who raises his head above the parapet is asking for trouble.

"The medical establishment's attitude to ending life is the same as a century ago. Radical change is needed. There should of course be adequate legal safeguards, and I would also like to see a religious service with hymns and the person in question surrounded by loved ones before being taken into a side room for a lethal injection. Suicide is a lonely and miserable end to someone's life. Why should an individual feel forced to take that option?"

[from an article by Elizabeth Udall, "My Life is so lonely", in *The Independent*, 7 December 1994]

Q

3 Do you think it is ethically right for a patient to ask a doctor to commit euthanasia?

4 Why does Dr Stephen Henderson Smith agree with euthanasia in some cases? Do you think he is correct?

Sample Examination Questions and Answers: Euthanasia

Total for questions [a], [b], and [c]: 20 marks

[a] Explain the meaning of the following terms and explain what the law in Britain says about them:
(i) voluntary euthanasia; (ii) involuntary euthanasia.
[5 marks]

[b] How might religious people respond to the viewpoint of the dying person? [10 marks]

[c] "Religion should be there to comfort the dying, but let the doctors make the decisions!"
How far do you agree with this comment? Give reasons to support your answer and show that you have thought about different points of view. [5 marks]

Q [a] ANSWER ONE – GRADE A

(i) Voluntary euthanasia is <u>when one person asks someone else to help them to die</u>, for example, if they were in <u>pain from cancer</u>.

Shows understanding.

Gives example.

(ii) Involuntary euthanasia is <u>when somebody helps someone to die without them being aware of it</u>. Examples of this include someone on a life support machine who is nearly brain dead, and <u>relatives decide it would be better for the machine to be switched off</u>. Euthanasia is <u>illegal in Britain</u>.

Clearly understands and gives example.

Legal position.

Q [a] ANSWER TWO – GRADE C

(i) Voluntary euthanasia is where someone who is <u>terminally ill</u> and has no chance of getting better decides that they would rather die now than wait for a long, slow, painful and undignified death. <u>This person may then ask a close friend, relative or the doctor to help them die sooner.</u>

Gives example.

Explains voluntary euthanasia.

(ii) Involuntary euthanasia is where someone does not ask for help to die because they can't. It would be involuntary euthanasia <u>to turn the life support machine off if the patient has not agreed</u>.

Second type explained but not developed.

No answer on legal position.

Q [b] ANSWER ONE – GRADE A

Religious attitudes towards euthanasia vary. The Bible states clearly that we were <u>created in the image of God; that life is valuable and God given; that God gives and that God will take away; that God gives life so there is dignity in it</u>. All of these arguments plus the commandment "Thou shall not kill" could be used by a religious person to encourage a person to live on. Also there is the argument that <u>God has a purpose for suffering</u> and that life now is as important as life in an afterlife. We should not destroy what God has made.

However, other religious people may <u>interpret the Bible in a different way</u>, arguing that the commandment "Thou shall not kill" is referring to murder and not to euthanasia. They may argue that by letting someone die in what they consider a dignified manner is showing <u>compassion and agape (love)</u>. Some Christians may argue that, <u>as long as the intention is not to harm the person but to help them</u>, then euthanasia is allowed and God would wish us to help someone get over their suffering.

Some Christians, such as Mother Teresa, would argue euthanasia isn't necessary as movements such as <u>hospices</u> which look after the spiritual and physical welfare of the dying have been set up. <u>Mother Teresa argued that just as Christ showed his love to the sick and dying, we should show how unselfish we are by making the last days of dying people's lives worthwhile.</u> Many Christians believe there is a reason for our existence and even if we do not know it now, it will become clear in life with God.

Focuses clearly on the question.

Purpose for suffering.

Alternative view.

Good reference to the work of hospices.

Excellent references.

Clear understanding of the issues.

Diversity of opinion.

Technical language.

Example of Christian action.

Diversity of opinion.

Q [b] ANSWER TWO – GRADE C

Christians differ on this issue and it is difficult to know which is the right thing to do. Some Christians say that keeping someone alive by drugs or a life support machine when they would otherwise die is wrong, if the person doesn't want it. If the person is dying and does not want to wait for a slow and painful death then many Christians would agree that it is only right for them to have the life support machine turned off or the medicine stopped. Christians might also argue that such *Argument for euthanasia.* artificial aids are only prolonging death and that God may have wished them to die but modern technology is keeping them alive. It is also a Christian view that the kindest thing to do is to put the patient out of their pain and misery.

Purpose for suffering. Other Christians say that euthanasia is very wrong. They argue that a person's suffering is purposeful and God has intended it. If God wants a person to die then they would be dead, and if you help someone to die then you are going against God's will. Doctors shouldn't have the right to play God.

In conclusion I think Christians would say that euthanasia is wrong but so is keeping someone alive when they should be dead.

Contains broad generalisations. Lacks response to stimulus but concentrates on arguments for and against euthanasia. Lacks religious teachings and ideas.

Understanding of the issues.

Recognises role of both religion and doctors.

Q [c] ANSWER ONE – GRADE A

Both religion and the medical profession should be there to comfort and help the dying. Those who believe in God find much strength in the thought of an afterlife with him and this may help them through their pain and the fear of leaving this life. Also we have come to rely very heavily on doctors, and in many ways I would argue doctors can take away pain through drugs, as religion can through providing strength.

Strength from belief. Help from medical profession.

Biblical reference. The danger arises if the doctors decide to play God and end life. Many Christians would argue that "God gives life and God should take it away." Decisions about ending a life should not just be in the hands of doctors because it could be abused. Others may disagree with me and say that the doctors are the professionals and *Good evaluation supported with sound reasoning. Balanced argument. Realises the complexity of the issues.* know when it is right to make difficult decisions. Christians are likely to point out that people can go to hospices to die, thanks to the work of people like Dame Cicily Saunders. Here they are surrounded by love and care and they can receive religious comfort in the final days of their lives.

Good example.

Personally, if I were dying, I would want doctors about trying to find new cures for my disease and also giving me comfort, as well as religious people praying for my recovery.

Sound personal response.

Q [c] ANSWER TWO – GRADE C

I agree with this statement as long as it is saying that the doctors can make the decisions outside of today's British law, i.e. they can do what they think is best personally for every patient. Religion is a great comforter for the dying because it reassures them that although they are leaving their family and friends they are going to a better place. The reason why I agree with this statement is because the doctors *Recognises doctors are medical experts.* know what their patient's chance of survival is, and they are in the best position to judge if a person will die or not. The only extent to which I don't agree with this statement is when doctors decide to keep people alive when they have no chance of survival and it is against their own and their families' wishes. I think in cases like that they should have the choice on whether they want to die or not.

Recognises role of religion to comfort.

Gives personal opinion.

Lacks religious teaching. The answer is one-sided.

War and Peace: What the Religions Say

BUDDHISM

"I will harm no living thing." [1st Precept]

"Laying aside the cudgel and the sword he dwells compassionate and kind to all living creatures." [Digha Nikaya 1.4]

CHRISTIANITY

"Love your enemies and pray for those who persecute you." [Matthew 5: 44]

"You have heard that it was said, 'Eye for eye, and tooth for tooth.' But I tell you, Do not resist an evil person. If someone strikes you on the right cheek, turn to him the other also." [Matthew 5: 38-39]

"For all who draw the sword will die by the sword." [Matthew 26: 52]

HINDUISM

"Ahimsa is the highest dharma . . . Ahimsa is the greatest gift. Ahimsa is the highest self-control. Ahimsa is the highest sacrifice. Ahimsa is the highest power. Ahimsa is the highest friend. Ahimsa is the highest truth. Ahimsa is the highest teaching." [Mahabharata XVIII: 116.37-41]

"What is virtuous conduct? It is never destroying life, for killing leads to every other sin." [Tirukural, verse 321]

Fighting is allowed in order to maintain a peaceful society: "If you do not fight in this just war, you will neglect your duty, harm your reputation and commit the sin of omission. Having regard to your duty, you should not hesitate, because for a warrior there is nothing greater than a just war." [Bhagavad Gita 2: 31 and 33]

ISLAM

"Fight in the cause of Allah those who fight you, but do not transgress limits . . . if they cease, let there be no hostility except to those who practise oppression." [Qur'an, 2: 190, 193]

"Paradise is for those who curb their anger and forgive their fellow men." [Qur'an, 3: 134]

"Hate your enemy mildly; he may become your friend one day." [Hadith]

JUDAISM

Peace is an ideal: "The Torah was given to establish peace." [Midrash]

"If our enemy is hungry, give him bread to eat; if he is thirsty, give him water to drink." [Proverbs 25: 21]

But war is allowed in certain circumstances: "The Lord said to Joshua, 'Rise, up, cross over this River Jordan, you and all this nation. Every place where the sole of your foot treads I will give to you. Be strong and courageous, for you will lead this people to take possession of the land which I have promised." [Joshua 1: 2]

SIKHISM

"The Khalsa – pure ones – shall rule, no hostile powers shall exist ... Those who enter the Khalsa for shelter will be protected. Without power, justice does not flourish, without justice everything is crushed." [Dasam Granth]

"When all efforts to restore peace prove useless and no words avail, lawful is the flash of steel, it is right to draw the sword." [Guru Gobind Singh]

1 Use the *Thinking Through Religion* textbook to collect teachings of the religions on non-violence and peace. What do the teachings have in common? Why do you think peace is such an important concept to religions?

2 Which religions believe that war is sometimes justified?

3 If religions preach peace, why do you think they sometimes support wars?

With God on our side!

In 1963 the musician Bob Dylan wrote a song called "With God on our side". In it he described how so many people go to war believing that God is on their side. Throughout history, countries have been torn apart by wars carried out in the name of religion. This continues today.

Fighting breaks out between Christians and Muslims in the Nigerian town of Ilorin [January 2000]

Sunni Muslims in Afghanistan poised for holy war against Shia Muslims in Iran [September 1998]

Israel declares war on Islamic Ummah

Christians in Pakistan demonstrate against rise of Hindu fundamentalism and attacks on Indian Christians [January 1999]

Why do people fight each other in the name of religion? Here are some viewpoints:

(a) "Many religious people believe that God has given them a mandate to convert others. It is a matter of trying to save their souls. If you believe that a person is in danger of eternal punishment if they do not belong to your religion, then you would be willing to try everything – even fighting – in order to convert them."

(b) "Religious people believe that all the world needs to be brought under God's control. Muslims talk about 'submission to Allah', Christians talk about 'establishing God's Kingdom'. If they have to achieve this by force, they will."

(c) "People who go to war in the name of religion are using God for their own ends. All religions teach that God wishes for peace and harmony. So how can religious people believe that God desires war?"

(d) "Religious people are still only people – they still do things wrong, and war is wrong, no matter how it is justified."

(e) "If you read some religious scriptures you will discover that God encourages believers to go to war to crush their enemies. Just look at the Bible where God encourages the Hebrews to attack the Amalekites."

Muslim-Christian religious war threatens Indonesian islands

Thousands of Muslim protesters have taken to the streets of the Indonesian capital, Jakarta, demanding a jihad, or holy war, to protect their fellow Muslims in the Spice Islands of Indonesia (the Moluccas). "The holy war is an obligation for us Muslims against people who attack us." For the last twelve months Christians and Muslims have massacred each other, burned down churches and mosques, and looted each other's property.

[January 2000]

1 Choose one of the conflicts from those mentioned in the news headlines and research it, perhaps on the Internet. Try to discover why people are fighting each other. What do they believe?

2 Which of the opinions quoted do you (a) most agree with; (b) disagree with? Explain why.

3 What is a holy war? Do you think war can ever be holy?

4 Sometimes you will hear it said that religious issues are at the root of many wars. Why do you think people are sometimes so passionate about their religion that they are willing to fight in order to protect it?

The madness of war

Ahimsa, non-violence, is a central ethical principle in a number of religions, including Buddhism. This sheet explores an extreme form of non-violent protest against the horrors of war. It looks at how a number of Buddhist monks and nuns harmed themselves as a form of non-violent protest. They acted in what many would term a "mad" way in order to draw the world's attention to the madness of war.

BUDDHIST MONKS AND NUNS BURN THEMSELVES IN PROTEST

In Saigon, Vietnam, on 11 June 1963, Thich Quang Duc, an elderly Buddhist monk, walked to a busy main road intersection. A large crowd watched as two other monks poured petrol over him and Quang Duc lit a match. He burned to death over the course of a few moments, sitting calmly in the lotus position. In the air was the smell of burning flesh. As he burned, Quang Duc never moved a muscle nor uttered a word. A press photographer caught his horrible death on film, and the photograph appeared on the front pages of newspapers all over the world.

Thich Quang Duc was the first of four Buddhist monks who took their own lives in this way between 1963 and 1975. In 1966, Nhat Chi Mai, a Buddhist nun, burned herself alive at the Tu Nghiem Temple. She left behind letters to the Presidents of North and South Vietnam, begging them to stop the fighting which had been going on between North and South since 1959.

What motivated these people to kill themselves? The first main explanation was that they were protesting against religious persecution. In protest against religious persecution of Buddhists in South Vietnam, Buddhists had submitted five requests to the government: (1) to lift the ban on flying the traditional Buddhist flag; (2) to grant Buddhists the same rights as Catholic Christians; (3) to stop holding Buddhists as prisoners for no reason; (4) to give Buddhist monks and nuns the right to practise and spread their religion; and (5) to pay fair compensation to victims' families and punish those responsible for their deaths.

The second explanation was that the Buddhist monks and nuns killed themselves as a protest against the American-backed war which was tearing Vietnam apart. They thought that the horrific manner of their deaths would draw world attention to the horror of the war, and this would then put pressure on their own governments to bring an end to the slaughter.

The death of Quang Duc had a powerful influence on events in South Vietnam in 1963. Many people believe that the fall of the South Vietnamese government in that year was linked to the Buddhist protests. Buddhists interpret these deaths as part of the Buddhist struggle for peace during the Vietnam War (1959-75). During the war Buddhists tried not to take sides, but instead to protest against the chaos of war.

1 What do you think of this story?

2 Many Buddhists interpret the monks' actions as examples of non-violence awakening the world to the suffering caused by the Vietnam War and the persecution of Buddhists. During the war Buddhists practised many other acts of non-violence, such as fasting and sitting calmly before an advancing tank – in an attempt to meet violence with ways of peace. Do you think non-violence is a good way of responding to violence?

3 The deaths of the Buddhist monks had political consequences. Was theirs an act of selflessness – to take their own life in order to save others?

4 At the heart of Buddhist ethical teaching is the prohibition on taking life and, in particular, on suicide. How do you think these Buddhist monks could justify their action? Is it a case of drastic action being necessary in times of war?

Sample Examination Questions and Answers: War and Peace

Total for questions [a], [b], and [c]: 20 marks

[a] Explain the conditions which need to be met for a Just War. [7 marks]

[b] Some religious people are prepared to fight in a Just War. Others may be pacifists. Explain the religious ideas that might lead people to be pacifists. [8 marks]

[c] "Surely you wouldn't choose to be a soldier if you're religious."
How far do you agree with this comment? Give reasons to support your answer and show that you have thought about different points of view. [5 marks]

Q [a] ANSWER ONE – GRADE A

Condition plus explanation.

In a Just War you need prior declaration of an attack by the government of the country, and a just cause, e.g. to prevent genocide or to defend an ally. Also it should be used as a last resort, when all other means (for example, negotiations and trade sanctions) have been tried and failed. There must be proportionality with only the necessary force being used, and civilian immunity must be upheld. For example, it would be wrong to use an atomic bomb to blow up a village because a few rebels were hiding there. There should be a reasonable hope of success, and right attitudes – i.e. revenge must not be a motive. The war should promote good and try to remove evil. Many would argue that the Second World War was a Just War because of the desire to stop an evil man, Hitler, from wiping out the Jews and other people he didn't like.

Detail given to explain condition.

Again, condition explained with an example.

More conditions.

An example of so-called Just War.

Q [a] ANSWER TWO – GRADE C

Clearly identifies four conditions.

Centuries ago criteria for Just War were produced and had to be followed in order for a war to commence.

(i)   War must be a last resort. Everything else has to have been tried.
(ii)   Innocent civilians must not be killed during a battle.
(iii)   The war must be fought for right reasons. Revenge is not a good enough motive.
(iv)   Leaders of countries in battle must be aware of the war.
(v)   The war must be used to promote good and defeat evil.

Lacks detailed explanation.

Not completely accurate.

Q [b] ANSWER ONE – GRADE A

Pacifists believe that violence must be avoided, and many Christians, e.g. Quakers, also believe this and will not even fight in a "Just War". This is due to the Biblical teaching which states that you must "Love thy neighbour as you love yourself" and also that "Wisdom does more good than weapons." Also in the Ten Commandments God said: "Do not murder" and by going to war people will murder other people. Jesus' message through his life was that of peace and reconciliation, not of violence and bloodshed. He said, "Those who take the sword will die by the sword," and he encouraged his followers to "turn the other cheek".

Identifies denomination.

Includes five good biblical references.

Pragmatic pacifists believe that fighting is evil and that to get something good you must do something good, therefore war is not an option. Hence all of these religious ideas may lead a person to become a pacifist and campaign, like the Rev. Bruce Kent, against the production of weapons of violence such as nuclear bombs.

Good modern example.

Q [b] ANSWER TWO – GRADE C

Religious ideas that may lead to people becoming pacifists include the fact that war is wrong and messages like "Fighting never solves anything".

Many other biblical examples or modern examples could have been included.

The <u>Bible states that killing is wrong, in the Ten Commandments</u>. Jesus also refused to fight when he was arrested and said, "<u>Those who take the sword will die by the sword</u>." Gruelling pictures of war and many war films that have been made may put people off fighting in another war. <u>War causes death, destruction, refugees and cripples</u>. How could a Christian support that, as war is an evil. <u>Jesus was for love and compassion, not hate and violence</u>.

Includes biblical references.

Good general point.

Example of Jesus.

Q [c] ANSWER ONE – GRADE A

Shows a sound ability to think through the issues, and attempts to balance the argument.

I don't totally agree, because in Judaism, religious men (except ultra Orthodox Jews) do become soldiers because it is part of <u>their belief and covenant with God to protect the land He gave them</u>. In the war between Israelites and some of their Arab neighbours, they are fighting over land, and during the making of the covenant the deal was that God gave the Jews land, but they must live in it and follow His teachings. Although Jews don't like to fight, they feel they must do so to keep the covenant and survive as a nation.

Good reference to situation in the Middle East.

Reference to Paul's teaching.

Good examples.

Also, being religious doesn't necessarily mean you're a pacifist. <u>You can still want to fight for your country and Queen and obey the Law of your country (as instructed by Paul in his letter to the Romans)</u>. Also you may be standing up for what is right e.g. in a Just War and fighting to end injustice. For example, <u>Bonhoeffer</u> decided he had to make a stand against Hitler. In South America some Christians believe in <u>Liberation Theology</u>.

However the main aspect of Christianity is to <u>treat others as you would like to be treated and love your fellow man</u>. Therefore by going to war and being a soldier you are breaking God's will.

Reference to Christian teaching.

If you are a pacifist you would probably agree with the statement but many religious people would disagree, believing that there are occasions when it is right to fight either physically or spiritually.

Q [c] ANSWER TWO – GRADE C

I agree with the statement. A religious person who believes in God and the teaching of Jesus should not go to war. The Ten Commandments say "<u>Thou Shalt not Kill</u>", and Jesus taught that we should turn the other cheek. <u>Jesus set an example for Christians</u> by riding peacefully into Jerusalem on a donkey, not a war horse, and he was prepared to die rather than resist arrest in the garden of Gethsemane.

Useful biblical reference.

Jesus' example.

On the other hand, it may be some <u>real injustice</u> that has driven you to fight, or you have to for your country or your family. Muslims might believe that it is a <u>Jihad and that they have to fight for Allah and their religion</u>.

Alternative view.

Reference to Jihad.

So ideally <u>I think</u> that religious people should not be members of the armed forces but there may be a few occasions when it might be seen as right to choose to be a soldier in order to right a wrong.

Personal opinion.

Planet Earth

"Green issues" are a popular subject amongst many teenagers, so there is great potential for debate and learning in this part of *Thinking Through Religion*. Green issues are constantly in the news. For example, during the writing of this book the following have produced lively discussion in the media: eco-warriors, the ethics of transporting animals over long distances, fox hunting, and GM crops.

Careful attention needs to be paid to what the issues actually are. We advise careful construction of questions in order that students have the opportunity to think thoroughly about the issues from different perspectives. For example, an interesting discussion can be had over the differences between animal rights, welfare, and liberation.

A note of warning: there is a tendency for scientific and religious understandings of the universe to become polarised in students' minds. We would encourage them to see that the Science/Religion debate has been conducted almost exclusively in the West, between Science and one single religious tradition – Christianity; and that modern developments within both Science and Christian theology have made many of the apparent differences disappear.

The chapter on How should we care for planet Earth? covers the following topics:

▶ The origins of life (scientific and religious views)
▶ Care of the planet (responses to environmental problems; pollution; the use, abuse, and conservation of natural resources; animal and plant extinction)
▶ Concepts of responsibility, stewardship, creation, and sanctity of life
▶ Human attitudes to animals (issues including vegetarianism, animal experiments, factory farming, hunting, and other aspects of animal rights)
▶ Differing religious responses to animal rights and the means of protecting those rights, including the application of sacred texts, religious principles, and statements by religious authorities

Examination candidates will be expected to:

▶ be aware of relevant religious teachings from sacred texts, religious principles, and contemporary religious leaders and organisations;
▶ demonstrate knowledge and understanding of the diversity of viewpoints held by believers within a single religious tradition;
▶ develop the ability to make reasoned and informed judgements about religious and, where appropriate, other responses to ethical issues.

Activity Sheet/Study Skills Sheet	Key concept for students to consider
13.1 Planet Earth: What the Religions Say	Quotations from six world religions.
13.2 Creation and Evolution: the Debate	Whether the conflict between Science and Religion is inevitable or whether scientific and religious explanations of the universe are complementary.
13.3 The Creation Story Another Way	How the origins of the universe might be explained, in a new version of the Genesis story.
13.4 An Animal Rights Activist	How far should a person go to protect animals?
13.5 "Frankenstein Foods"	The relationship between humans and the natural world. Do humans have a right to manipulate nature to their own ends?
13.6 Exam Questions and Answers*	Sample questions and graded answers on Planet Earth.

* See Grade Descriptions on page 124.

Planet Earth: What the Religions Say

BUDDHISM

"I will avoid taking life. I will try to show loving-kindness towards all creatures." [1st Precept]

"Whoever in this world destroys life . . . such a one interferes with their own progress in this very world." [Dhammapada 246-7]

CHRISTIANITY

"Then the Lord God placed the man in the Garden of Eden to cultivate it and guard it." [Genesis 2: 15]

"The Earth and all life on it is a gift from God given to us to share and develop, not to dominate and exploit . . . We have the responsibility to create a balanced policy between consumption and conservation." [Pope John Paul, Sollicitudo Rei Socialis, 1988]

"The dominion given to human beings over the natural order is that of stewards who have to render an account." [Church of England, motion agreed at the General Synod, 1992]

HINDUISM

"Now see, O Arjuna, in my body the entire Universe – movable and immovable – and whatever else you wish to see." [Krishna in the Bhagavad Gita 11: 7]

"There is said to be a network of pearls, arranged so that if you look at one you see all the others reflected in it. In the same way each object in the world is not merely itself but involves every other object, and in fact is every other object." [Flower Garland Sutra]

ISLAM

"All Creation is like a family of God; and He loves the most those who are the most beneficent to His family." [Hadith]

"The Earth is green and beautiful, and Allah has appointed you his stewards over it." [Qur'an, 6: 165]

JUDAISM

"The earth is the Lord's and all that it holds, the world and its inhabitants." [Psalm 24: 1]

"You appointed him ruler over everything you made; you placed him over all creation." [Psalm 8: 6]

"When in your war against a city you have to besiege it a long time in order to capture it, you must not destroy its trees, wielding the axe against them. You may eat them, but you must not cut them down." [Deuteronomy 20: 19]

SIKHISM

"You, Lord, are the river wherein all things dwell; apart from you nothing can be. All that has life owes that life to your purpose ... Wondrous Creator, the Maker of all things, apart from you nothing can be." [Evening Prayer]

"The Lord pervades all created beings; God creates all and assigns all their tasks." [Guru Granth Sahib 434]

"In Nature we see God, In Nature we hear God speak, Nature inspires devotion, In Nature is the essence of joy and peace." [Guru Granth Sahib 464]

1 What ideas do the religions share?

2 How does each religion view God in relation to the world? How do the religions differ in their views on this subject?

Creation and Evolution: the Debate

Charles Darwin (1809-82) was a scientist. He is known most for the theory of evolution. He suggested a mechanism – natural selection – by which new species evolve from existing ones. Species which adapt to changing environments survive. When species cannot adapt, like the dinosaurs, they become extinct. Darwin believed that life forms have developed from very simple structures to the complex and intricate forms we have today. His theory seemed to argue against the idea that God was the great intelligent designer responsible for all the detail and ordered structure in the universe.

1   There is still lively debate about whether the world was created or whether it evolved. On this sheet are opinions from both sides. Divide a page into two columns and collect arguments from the opinions here into "Arguments for Creation" and "Arguments for Evolution".

2   Do you think it is possible to accept both the argument from design and the theory of evolution? Explain your answer.

"God arranged the whole universe to provide the conditions necessary for life to evolve. Evolution is the science that studies how God created the species."
[Victoria, interview with author]

"In the years after Darwin published his findings, tens of thousands of Christians left their churches because they could no longer believe in God. Today, almost all Christians accept natural selection and do not find this in any way incompatible with belief in God. It can be argued that natural selection itself might be the mechanism that God uses to bring about His purposes. Darwin recognised that natural selection did not explain everything."
[Peter Vardy, *The Puzzle of God*, Fount, 1995]

"[You must] distinguish between microevolution [small developments within the species], and macroevolution [the process which creates new complex organs or new body parts]. Scientists have evidence for microevolution but not for macroevolution . . . the fossil record overall is extremely disappointing to Darwinian expectations. One prime example is the 'Cambrian explosion', where the basic animal groups all appear suddenly and without evidence of evolutionary ancestors."
[adapted from Philip E. Johnson, *Defeating Darwinism*, IVP, 1997]

"If Darwin was right in thinking that species formed by a process of natural selection which protected the survival of the fittest, how do you explain the selfless acts of animals and people, when they protect the weak members of their species? Why do people care for the handicapped and mentally ill? Where do they get this moral sense from?"
[Clarence, interview with author]

The Creation Story Another Way

If the Creation Story were written today, says Professor E. J. Burge, it would be very different from the familiar and ancient story in Genesis. But the divine truths would be the same. Here is his modern (January 2000) version.

TODAY'S CREATION STORY

IN THE BEGINNING, God said, "Let there be ...", and he created the unified forces of physics, with perfect symmetry, and prescient precision.

And out of nothing, and into nothing, God, by a free decision, set up the spontaneous production of particles, in new-born space and time, producing a silent, seething sphere, infinitesimally small, and unimaginably hot.

There was evolution and emergence, the first stage of Creation.

DURING a tiny fraction of a second, an expansion took place, and the perfect symmetry of the forces was broken, step by step, as the temperature dropped, to produce the forces of nature we know today.

God's well-tuned laws made innumerable particles of every requisite kind, in a steadily expanding chaotic cooling sphere. And the universe cooled for nearly a million years, until electrons could stay joined to nuclei to form familiar atoms.

There was evolution and emergence, the second stage of Creation.

WITH ATOMS and molecules as building blocks, the attracting force of gravity took over, and after about a thousand million years, God saw the first stars and galaxies forming in an expanding cosmic Universe.

There was evolution and emergence, the third stage of Creation.

INDIVIDUAL stars contracted under gravity, and became hot enough for nuclear fusion to produce chemical elements not seen before, until, after about ten thousand million years, stars were exhausted by their radiance, and God saw them begin to die, some dramatically, by exploding as supernovae, releasing all the known chemical elements.

There was evolution and emergence, the fourth stage of Creation.

AND GOD SAW that it was very good, for now all the ingredients were available, and gravity formed a second generation of stars, some accompanied by planets and satellites, including the Sun, Earth and, later, the Moon, in our Galaxy of the Milky Way.

There was evolution and emergence, the fifth stage of Creation.

BATHED in alternate daylight and darkness, during the next thousand million years or so, conditions on Earth became favourable for the eventual generation of life.

There was evolution and emergence, the sixth stage of Creation.

DURING these last three thousand million years, life has evolved as God intended, and through numerous cycles of birth, survival, procreation and death, species have multiplied and progressed, plants and animals of every kind, and some have become extinct, until, a mere three hundred thousand years ago, there arrived, in the likeness of God, homo sapiens, intelligent humans, with freedom to choose, living together in community, knowing good and evil, pleasure and pain, aware of honour due to their dominion, and acquainted with death.

There was evolution and emergence, the seventh stage of Creation, and the Universe entered the Age of Humanity.

HUMAN BEINGS have hardly changed in physical form, during the last forty thousand years, but their beliefs have evolved, their knowledge has grown, and their understanding has deepened.

And God saw that it was good, but it was not good enough, for free will led to sin and suffering, and guilt and disbelief could lead to despair and the death of the human spirit.

So God sent his only Son, the Word made flesh, who dwelt among us, as Jesus of Nazareth, suffered, died and rose from the dead, and showed his glory, full of grace and truth.

And that was the beginning of the New Creation.

1 Compare Professor Burge's account of creation with that found in Genesis 1. What are the similarities and differences? What is missing? Why?

2 Describe how Professor Burge believes God created the world through the process of evolution.

3 Do you think it is possible to believe in both the theories of creation and evolution?

An Animal Rights Activist

ANIMAL ACTIVIST ON HUNGER STRIKE

[Thursday, 26 November 1998]

Last night Barry Horne was on his deathbed. It is the third time he has been on hunger strike since he was sent to jail in 1996. Barry is a man who puts animals' lives before his own.

Barry has been an animal lover and activist for all his adult life. In September 1988 he was fined £500 and given a six-month suspended sentence for conspiring to steal a dolphin from an aquarium in Morecombe. In 1995 the police raided his flat and found pamphlets supporting attacks on shops with "miraculously igniting cigarette packets". In 1996 he was sentenced to 18 years in jail for arson. Barry had firebombed a shop that sold guns to shoot wildlife. The shop was empty and no one was hurt.

Judge Simon Darwall-Smith told him: "This was urban terrorism for a particular cause by which you put communities in terror." Detective Chief Inspector Roy Lambert said: "This man was not going to let anything come in his way. His history shows he is a truly dedicated animal rights activist. He never gave a moment's thought about any loss of life that may have occurred." Police found six incendiary devices at his home and four in his jacket: Superking cigarette packets stuffed with a watch timer and explosives.

Barry began his hunger strikes last year, in protest at broken promises by the government. The first lasted 35 days. The second lasted 46 days. His third hunger strike started 50 days ago. This time he is striking until the government promises to set up a Royal Commission on vivisection. However, Home Office Minister George Howarth has said that the government won't give in to "blackmail".

On the early morning of 13th November, activists sprayed 79 walls in London with slogans like "Support Barry Horne hunger strike", "stop vivisection", etc. Barry has signed a living will stating that he wants no medical help if he loses consciousness.

"Fighting for the animals"

Barry Horne explained the reason for his action in a letter written on Day 1 of his hunger strike, 6 October 1998:

"The fight is not for us, not for our personal wants and needs. It is for every animal that has suffered and died in the vivisection labs, and for every animal that will suffer and die in those same labs unless we end this evil business now! The souls of the tortured dead cry for justice, the cry of the living is for freedom. We can create that justice and we can deliver that freedom. The animals have no-one but us, we will not fail them."

On Day 6 of his hunger strike, 11 October, he wrote:

"I'm feeling exhausted all the time, weak, nauseous and light-headed. Whatever . . . my morale is high. As is my determination to see this protest through to a successful conclusion. The animals demand nothing less, and I won't let them down."

1   In the end, Barry Horne ended his hunger strike. What questions would you like to ask him if you could interview him?

2   What do his actions tell you about his beliefs?

3   Do you think his actions are moral/ethical?

"Frankenstein Foods"

Scare over GM Foods

[February 1999]

Freshness in the genes

So what are GM (genetically modified) foods and why have them? Take, as one example, the average garden tomato. As you know, it lasts only a few days before it starts to go off. Most tomatoes are like that, because it is in their genes. But scientists have been able to identify the genes in certain varieties of tomato which lengthen their keeping qualities. Transplanting these genes into the average tomato-types makes them last longer too. That is an example of genetic modification to improve the shelf-life of a product.

GM products like that make sense for supermarkets wanting to increase their profits. When fresh fruit and vegetables begin to go off, the shop has to reduce their price and eventually throw some of them away. The longer the fruit and vegetables stay fresh, the more money the shop can make.

Suddenly it's monstrous

GM foods have been growing in number for years. But it is only recently that people have become aware of this and started to question whether they can trust in such scientific developments. Some people are calling GM food "Frankenstein food". Frankenstein is the name of a character in a novel by Mary Shelley. He brilliantly creates a human-like being, who then torments Frankenstein and causes disaster. People now are suggesting that the food that scientists create, using their knowledge about genes,

might similarly prove to have disastrous consequences in future.

Recent reports suggest that wildlife which feeds on GM foods has a shortened lifespan. Laboratory tests showed that the lifespan of ladybirds that ate greenfly that had fed off GM crops was reduced by half.

Sterile seeds

Naturally, crops grown from seed produce new seeds and these can be planted and new crops will grow. It is a kind of recycling that saves gardeners and farmers money. Some seed companies in the West have used GM technology to produce sterile seeds which cannot be "recycled" in this way. This gives the companies power over their customers – who include farmers in the developing world.

On the other hand, people point out that GM technology will make it possible to grow more and better food crops, in particular for the developing world.

In 1999 the issue of GM foods and crops suddenly burst into the news. Environmental campaigners made the headlines by attacking fields where GM crops were being grown. They also demanded that all foods should be clearly labelled as to whether they included any GM ingredients. Supermarkets removed certain foods from sale and stated their policies about GM.

1   What is Genetic Modification? For what reasons might it be done? Who benefits or will benefit from it?

2   Why do you think environmental groups are campaigning for GM foods to be identified?

3   Do you think scientists have a right to alter nature?

4   Why might some religious traditions disagree with GM foods?

5   Are we creating monster foods and thus "playing at" being the Creator?

6   Sum up your views by writing a letter to your Member of Parliament.

Sample Examination Questions and Answers: Planet Earth

Total for questions [a], [b], and [c]: 20 marks

Read the poem on the right and answer the questions below.

[a] The poem lists some problems faced by the Earth. Choose one of these problems and explain how it harms the environment. [5 marks]

[b] Why would most religious people **not** agree that they can "do what they like" with the Earth? [10 marks]

[c] "Over the years, religions have said a lot about murder, stealing and greed. It would have been better to have said more about the environment."
How far do you agree with this comment? Give reasons to support your answer and show that you have thought about different points of view. [5 marks]

> **The Earth has Feelings!**
> You don't like *smelly cars*
> So why should I?
>
> You don't like *litter*
> So why should I?
>
> You don't like *pollution*
> So why should I?
>
> You don't like *nuclear weapons*
> So why should I?
>
> You think I'm yours to do as you please,
> But I'm not I'm me!

Answer clearly focused on the question.

Reference to global warming.

Q [a] ANSWER ONE – GRADE A

Smelly Cars. Cars emit carbon dioxide, sulphur dioxide, carbon monoxide, nitrogen dioxide and many other harmful gases and pollutants. The carbon dioxide adds to a build-up of the substance in the atmosphere, and can cause heat to be trapped in the atmosphere, resulting in global warming. Sulphur dioxide makes acid rain when it dissolves in the droplets of water in the atmosphere. Acid rain erodes buildings, kills wildlife, pollutes water supplies and destroys trees. Carbon monoxide is poisonous to human beings and so is a health risk. Nitrogen dioxide is another "greenhouse gas", acting like carbon dioxide. Cars also use fossil fuels (a non-renewable energy source) and some petrol contains lead which once in the atmosphere has harmful effects e.g. can damage children's brains.

Good introduction.

Cause and effects given.

Further problem explained.

Identifies some of the problems.

Mention of health risks.

Q [a] ANSWER TWO – GRADE C

"Smelly Cars" give out carbon dioxide and sulphur dioxide fumes. These combine with water vapour to form acid rain. Acid rain falls and causes great damage to buildings, eroding them, and especially to trees. If it falls into a river, pond or stream, then it poisons the water life, and can kill them. Carbon monoxide is poisonous to humans and is one of the causes of the greenhouse effect which is leading to climatic changes to the world and global warming.

Developed answer on acid rain.

Reference to climatic problems.

The Earth – God's creation.

Q [b] ANSWER ONE – GRADE A

Religious people would say that they are "stewards" on this Earth, that they should oversee, look after and respect nature and the environment. Also, they would say that God created all things on the Earth and Earth itself, and so all things on it should be respected. Just because we are powerful, more so than other creatures, we don't have the right to do with creatures as we wish. God created the Earth and animals first, before humans. He created us last and, according to Genesis, gave us the responsibility of looking after all creation. We can't do what we like with the Earth because it belongs to God and we are responsible to him for our actions. However, we were created with free will, and some Christians (particularly in America) argued

Idea of stewardship.

Reference to Genesis.

Diversity of belief.

Biblical reference.

Good modern quote.

that we can do with the Earth as we please. Most Christians would argue that we have a responsibility to look after the Earth, and the free will we were given is to test how we manage the Earth and how we treat other creatures. Loving our neighbour applies to animals as well as humans and Christians should follow the example of St Francis of Assisi who showed respect for all living creatures. Christianity (and the Pope who says "we must destroy laboratories of death") says that we should respect nature and give thanks to God for our world, not abuse the privilege of life.

Good example.

Q [b] ANSWER TWO – GRADE C

Most religious people including Christians and Sikhs would disagree with this statement, as they believe that the Earth is God's creation, and that we are stewards or custodians of it. God trusts us to keep it well, and we have abused his trust. Sikhs think that God is in everything, that if you chop down a tree, then you are destroying a piece of God. They also think that we should look after animals, since God put us in charge, and trusted us to be good.

Reference to God's creation, with use of technical terms.

Sikh belief.

General points.

Technical term.

If people believe that they can do what they like with the Earth, it encourages greed, and gluttony. These are in direct conflict with the command "Love thy neighbour". Greed is also one of the Deadly Sins. Such hatred and disregard of others' feelings is the opposite of agape love, which Christianity tries to promote.

Biblical reference.

Q [c] ANSWER ONE – GRADE A

I don't agree completely because the environmental concerns have only been realised over recent years, and problems like murder, stealing and greed have been going on since religions began. However, as soon as the truth about animals and abuse of nature were known, religion should perhaps have said more about these subjects.

Idea of modern issue.

Supports the statement.

Evaluates importance of murder, stealing and greed.

Murder, stealing and greed are all mentioned in the Ten Commandments, which form the basis of the laws for Christianity. But environmental issues were not so important when the Bible was written, although it states that the treatment of animals is important. Perhaps more emphasis could have been placed on the environment to avoid problems for the future.

I believe that the basis of the environmental problems is murder, stealing and greed. The murder of wildlife, the stealing of resources and the greed of people who pollute the world. It can be argued that all three are the root causes of the environmental problems and so, in a sense, religions have been addressing the issues – but perhaps they should have related them more fully to the environment.

Good argument realising the complexity of the issues.

Q [c] ANSWER TWO – GRADE C

Murder, stealing and greed are very serious and it is important for religions to point out the effects these things have on human society. You cannot love your neighbour and go around stealing from them or killing people, and so it is right that religions point this out. This was a major problem when religions such as Christianity and Sikhism began. Both religions have also emphasised the importance of looking after the world and living things, e.g. animals. So it is not true that environmental issues have been ignored. Most Sikhs are very aware of the need to protect life as they are taught that God is in all things.

Based on Christian teaching.

Inclusion of Sikh position.

Awareness that it is modern issue.

I agree that in Christianity environmental issues have not been a priority, probably because it is only in recent years that people have become more aware of the problems of pollution, global warming etc. Now there are Christian groups which have been set up to warn people of the dangers of ignoring the environment and doing what we please with it.

Christian action mentioned.

Religion in Action

Chapters 14, 15, and 16 of *Thinking Through Religion* are concerned with religious teachings regarding human relationships. We look at individual relationships; the effect of wealth and poverty on relationships between individuals and between nations; and prejudice and discrimination. Students should focus on how religious believers demonstrate their beliefs are demonstrated in action. The chapters cover:

Relationships

- Contemporary debate about trends in marriage and divorce, and attitudes towards human sexuality
- Religious attitudes to sex outside marriage
- The purpose and nature of marriage (including the concepts of commitment, responsibility, social contract, covenant, sacrament, sanctity of vows)
- Religious responses to the issues of love, parental involvement, and race in the choice of a partner
- Why marriages succeed and fail
- Religious and non-religious attitudes towards divorce and remarriage

Wealth and poverty

- Attitudes towards wealth and possessions
- The distribution of wealth
- Religious attitudes to use of wealth
- Conflict between religion and materialism
- Key concepts such as justice, stewardship, compassion, and rights and responsibilities
- Reasons why and ways in which religious believers care for the needy

Prejudice

- Range of types of prejudice and discrimination
- Reasons for prejudice and discrimination
- Responses to prejudice and discrimination
- Application of sacred texts, religious principles, and statements by religious authorities to prejudice and discrimination
- Key concepts including human dignity, equality, justice, community and social responsibility

Examination candidates will be expected to:

- understand the teachings of the religion(s) studied with regard to relationships in which people live;
- demonstrate how sacred texts, religious principles, and statements by religious authorities can be applied to human relationships;
- show they have considered the links between religion and action in the lives of believers;
- show they have considered and evaluated in depth their own responses to the area being studied.

Activity Sheet/Study Skills Sheet	Key concept for students to consider
14.1 Is marriage out of date?	The value of marriage.
14.2 Are you tolerant? Should you be?	Is tolerance a good quality by which to live?
14.3 Teenage Pregnancies	The place of sex in the lives of young people.
14.4 Adultery	The attitudes of Islam and other religions towards adultery.
14.5 Strangers' Wedding	Choosing a marriage partner. Is marriage a sacrament or a contract?
14.6 The Monks, the Woman, and the River	Sexuality (a Buddhist story).
14.7 Exam Questions and Answers*	Sample questions and graded answers on Religion and Relationships.
15.1 Wealth & Poverty: What the Religions Say	Quotations from six world religions.
15.2 Islamic Relief	The work of an Islamic relief organisation.
15.3 National Lottery Fever	The power of money.
15.4 Exam Questions and Answers*	Sample questions and graded answers on Wealth and Poverty.
16.1 Colour is good, Lord	The value of human differences.
16.2 The Case of Stephen Lawrence	The effects of racism. Lessons from the Macpherson Report.
16.3 Exam Questions and Answers*	Sample questions and graded answers on Religion and Prejudice.

* See Grade Descriptions on page 124. Candidates in the SEG exam may choose to offer coursework on these subjects. See pages 110 and 125.

Is marriage out of date?

Today more and more people are choosing not to get married. This sheet explores whether marriage is an out-of-date idea or still relevant for people living in the 21st century.

(a) "Marriage forms a stable bond in which to have children. It provides stability for the home. Children need both father and mother."

(b) "God created marriage and provided the rules on how to make it work. If we follow those rules, marriages work."

(c) "No, I don't think people need to get married in order to have a stable family life. What is marriage but a piece of paper? People can live happily together without a ceremony to show that they are married. Marriage shows commitment but so does love between two people who have been living together for a long time."

(d) "Marriage is important for children. It is the appropriate arena in which to teach children how to love each other, how to care about each other."

(e) "If two people are not intending to have children I see no reason for them to get married."

(f) "If people enter marriage with a 'let's give it a try, we can get out of it if it doesn't work', then it is most likely going to fail. It all depends on attitude."

(g) "Family is the foundation of a stable society, and marriage makes family stable. The breakdown of our societies is mainly due to the break-up of our marriages."

(h) "Marriage is a good way in which society holds people and their children together. Without the institution of marriage there would be less commitment."

(i) "Marriage doesn't work unless it is part of a whole organisation of extended family and community relationships. It's the whole thing which is important, not just the marriage."

(j) "Marriage is out-of-date in today's society which is constantly changing. Emotions and human relationships change all the time. It is unrealistic to expect two people to love each other for the rest of their lives."

1 In 1999, the Conservative Party leader, William Hague, insisted that a successful society was dependent upon a large number of people being in happy marriages. Do you agree with this?

2 Read the selection of opinions quoted on this sheet. Which do you (a) most agree with?; (b) most disagree with? Explain why.

3 Is it realistic in this day and age to expect two people to stay together for the rest of their lives?

4 How does the TV represent marriage? Do the media present marriage as an attractive option for people?

Are you tolerant? Should you be?

Do you think of yourself as a tolerant person? Are there things which you do not tolerate?

Tolerance is a relatively new concept, but today it is very fashionable. Consider what would happen if you started to speak out in public against people you think are in error: the unmarried couple living together; your 16-year-old friend who has just had an abortion; two of your friends who are homosexual . . . More likely than not, people would accuse you of being intolerant. No wonder religions are often thought to be out-of-date as they dare to speak out against what they see to be the evils of society!

And yet how does a person know what is "right"? In today's pluralistic world there is such a multitude of views, beliefs, values, and practices. Many people would say that there is no single "right" way among them. Truth is merely opinion – what is right for you may not be right for me. Therefore we need to learn to tolerate each other's views and ways of behaving. If we don't, we will live in constant conflict. This is why some people regard intolerance as the greatest wrong.

However, it is widely recognised that no moral person tolerates everything. For some, racism and sexism are intolerable. Others might not tolerate the injustice in the world between the rich and poor. And others again might focus on pornography on television and the internet as something they will not tolerate.

Religion is often seen as expressing intolerance – as when, for example, it speaks out against abortion clinics, or gay marriages. But it is not just religious belief that leads people to speak out against certain actions. For instance, environmental campaigners and feminists put forward their strong views.

Does anyone have the right to try to convert others to his or her view?

> "The problem is not the fact that religious believers speak out against things they see as wrong. All of us have beliefs which we should be proud to support. The problem is in the selection of their issues: they are always speaking out against the 'evils' of pornography, homosexuality, abortion, adultery, prostitution, but are amazingly silent most of the time about the evils of racism and third world hunger and debt. Sometimes religious people give the impression that they are only interested in getting their noses into other people's bedrooms!"
>
> [Richard, 37]

> "What is the difference between a genuinely tolerant society, and a morally bankrupt one, incapable of calling evil for what it is? Is Chesterton on to something when he says tolerance is the virtue of those who don't believe in anything?"
>
> [Daniel Taylor in *Christianity Today*, 11 January 1999]

Everything is right somewhere and nothing is right everywhere.

1   Is tolerance a good thing? Provide examples.

2   Are there things that people should not tolerate? Provide examples.

3   Religious believers speak of certain things as sins or prohibitions. Name three issues on which religions are sometimes regarded as intolerant. Why do you think they take this stance? Do you think they are right to do so?

4   "Religious intolerance has caused many conflicts." Discuss.

Teenage Pregnancies

Fury over Birth Control Implant

A PROPOSAL that girls as young as 10 could in the future be implanted with long-acting hormonal contraceptives sparked a row yesterday over the best way to tackle Britain's high rate of teenage pregnancies.

Professor John Guillebaud said that a highly effective hormonal implant, which has just received its European licence, would be "ideal" for young girls who are more likely than older women to forget to take the Pill or use a condom. But his proposal was attacked by anti-abortion and conservative family organisations.

The row centres on a Dutch-made device called Implanon, a rod of hormones, 5 centimetres long, that is inserted under the skin of the arm and lasts for three years. Professor Guillebaud said: "In the future, and as a social policy, when you have an area with a huge rate of teenage pregnancies you could go into a school, obviously with the consent of the parents, and fit this device so that everybody would start out not being able to have a baby. It could be fitted into girls once they have started their periods but before they have had sex – for instance, at the time when they were having their rubella jabs. As of now, Implanon might be used for young girls who are already sexually active and who have difficulty remembering to take the contraceptive pill."

Valerie Riches of Family Youth Concern said: "I think the whole idea is repugnant. It will give youngsters the go-ahead to engage in sexual intercourse at an even earlier age."

The family campaigner Victoria Gillick said: "This amounts to the spaying of young children. It is outrageous. It is the wholesale sterilisation of young children. It is chemical castration. It is repugnant."

Even the Family Planning Association distanced itself from the idea. Ann Weyman, the FPA's chief executive, said: "We believe girls should be encouraged to have the self-confidence to take control of their lives and make responsible decisions about relationships. Contraception has to be viewed within this broader context."

[Based on a report in *The Independent*, 3 February 1999]

Rise in Teenage Pregnancies in the UK

THERE has been an increase of 11 per cent in the number of teenage girls becoming pregnant. The conception rate for girls aged 13 to 15 rose to 9.4 pregnancies per 1000 in 1996, compared with 8.5 in 1995, according to figures from the Office for National Statistics. More than three-quarters of the pregnant girls were 15 year-olds, and more than half had abortions.

There were 63 pregnancies per 1000 15-19 year-olds, two thirds of whom have their babies.

[Figures published in 1998 and 1999]

1   In a group, make a list of the issues involved in the story about the birth control implant.

2   Would the use of the implant encourage more young people to become sexually active sooner?

3   Professor Guillebaud suggested that the treatment take place in school. In some schools today contraceptives are available for sale. What messages do you think it gives to teenagers when contraceptives are available in school? Do you think contraceptives should be made available at school?

4   Professor Guillebaud says that this hormonal treatment will become a matter of social policy. Do you think the control of pregnancies is (a) a social issue, (b) a personal issue, (c) an economic issue?

5   Do you think Professor Guillebaud's recommendations are a good thing? Do you think they will happen?

Hume calls for an end to society's sexual obsession

SOCIETY should end its obsession with sex, eliminate pornography and put sexual intimacy back in its proper place of marriage, Cardinal Basil Hume, head of the Roman Catholic Church in England and Wales, said yesterday. There was a need to reflect on marriage and the family, and the role of sex, if there was to be any understanding of the root cause of abortion . . . The advent of the Pill in the Sixties had, paradoxically, led to an epidemic of unwanted pregnancies, many of which were terminated. "We have tried . . . to disconnect sex from child-bearing . . . the result has been a disaster. Paradoxically, the increase in contraception has been accompanied by a rise in abortion," he said.

[*Sunday Telegraph*, 21 March 1999]

Adultery

In March 1997, the Taliban Islamic movement in Afghanistan stoned to death a young woman for committing adultery. Later in that year, six people in Iran were stoned to death in public, after a court had found them guilty of adultery and prostitution. In November 1998, news reports from Iran told the story of another man who had been condemned to death by stoning for committing adultery. Because this man managed to free himself as the stoning was being carried out, he was acquitted of the crime.

A woman or man condemned to punishment by stoning is buried to the waist or neck and covered with a white sheet. She or he is then pelted with stones which, according to Article 119 of the Law of Hodoud and Qesas, "should not be too large so that the person dies on being hit by one or two of them; they should not be so small either that they could not be defined as stones."

Stoning is condemned by the non-Islamic world. Human rights groups point to article 5 of the Universal Declaration of Human Rights which states that "No one shall be subjected to torture or to cruel, inhuman or degrading treatment or punishment." They argue that stoning people to a slow and gradual death constitutes torture and degrading punishment.

The Islamic Republic of Iran has come under pressure from human rights groups both in and outside the country to stop death by stoning. Since the election of the reformist President Mohammad Khatami in May 1998, the number of stonings has fallen sharply, and other methods of execution have been used. Khatami won the election on his promise to create a "civil society".

However, execution is allowed in Islamic law. Therefore it can never be overturned as a punishment.

Adulterous wife stoned to death [March 1997]

Iran stops stoning to death [June 1998]

Q

1   What is the Islamic punishment for adultery? Why do you think Islam enforces such a harsh punishment for adultery?

2   Why are human rights groups opposed to stoning? Do you think they would feel the same about other methods of execution?

3   Why do you think all religions consider adultery harmful?

4   Do you think people should be punished for committing adultery? If so, how?

Strangers' Wedding

A Birmingham radio station, BRMB, recently ran a competition entitled "Two Strangers and a Wedding". The prize for the male and female winners was a blind-date marriage. The couple met for the first time minutes before their wedding ceremony, which was provided and arranged by the radio station.

Before the wedding, church leaders wrote to BRMB to express "profound concern" over the competition. The Archdeacon of Aston, the Venerable John Barton, said that it had turned "a solemn but wonderful institution ordained by God into a game show with prizes".

The Labour MP for Birmingham Erdington said the prize wedding was "degrading" and "a publicity stunt".

Mike Owen, head of BRMB publicity, spoke in support of the competition: "We have taken it all very seriously. We think this will be the ultimate failsafe arranged marriage." The couple were chosen from more than 200 candidates. Through a process of interviews a short list was arrived at of 12 candidates, who had to undergo more rigorous interviews, including a lie-detector test, as well as checks on astrological charts and interviews with family and friends.

1. What are your first thoughts about this blind-date marriage? In what sense is it an arranged marriage? How does the way it was arranged differ from the way some religions arrange a marriage?

2. Why did some people express "profound concern" over this form of marriage making?

3. Some people might argue that all marriages are arranged in one way or another. Who influences the choice of marriage partners? Why do you think many people in the Western world use dating agencies?

4. (a) Who would you trust to arrange a marriage for you: your parents, friends, and religion?
   (b) What factors would you like them to take into consideration before choosing a partner for you?
   (c) Why did the radio station use a lie detector and check astrological charts?

5. Do you think that finding the "right" person will automatically make you happy? What else might you need?

The Monks, the Woman, and the River

Two monks on a journey came to a river bank. There they met a beautiful young woman who, like them, needed to cross to the other side. The water, however, was very deep. The elder monk picked up the woman, carried her across the river, and put her down on the opposite bank. The two monks went on their way together.

It was obvious to the elder monk that the younger monk was anxious. After walking a few miles further, the younger monk finally broke the silence.

"Have you forgotten that you are a monk? What could you possibly be thinking about, picking up that beautiful woman and carrying her across the river?"

"I put the woman down at the edge of the river," replied the elder monk. "You are still carrying her".

1 In what sense was the younger monk still carrying the woman?

2 What is this spiritual story teaching about sexuality?

3 Which religious tradition do you think this story comes from? Explain your choice.

Sample Examination Questions and Answers: Religion and Relationships

Total for questions [a], [b], and [c]: 20 marks

[a] Explain the different causes of marriages breaking down today. [5 marks]

[b] Explain the religious views and teachings on divorce. [10 marks]

[c] "There should be a religious ceremony to end marriage in the same way that there is one to start it." How far do you agree with this idea? Give reasons to support your answer and show that you have thought about different points of view. [5 marks]

Q [a] ANSWER ONE – GRADE A

Reason for breakdown.

There are many different causes of marriage breakdowns today, such as <u>one member of the partnership having an affair</u> with someone else. <u>Children</u> may cause the breakdown in two ways: if a couple are unable to have children this can cause strain and friction and, on the other hand, the stresses of having children may have the same effect on a marriage.

Discussion of children developed.

Discussion of finance developed.

Answer clearly focused on the question.

   <u>Money problems resulting from such things as unemployment</u> may cause a breakdown. <u>The couple can end up quarrelling and falling out over what they can and can't spend etc</u>. If the couple <u>do not communicate and grow apart</u>, this can lead to a breakdown of the marriage. Also, <u>if the decision to get married was taken too lightly, regret and resentment may later cause a breakdown</u>.

Further reasons.

Q [a] ANSWER TWO – GRADE C

The problems faced today with regards to marriage breakdown are too numerous to mention. Reasons for the end of a marriage range from <u>adultery</u> to the man not putting the toilet seat down! It may sound stupid, but reasons can be as petty as that, although some can be serious such as <u>violent behaviour</u>. The main cause, however, is usually that <u>the couple fall out of love</u>. Marriage has become too commonplace in today's society. People think that they're in love, rush out and get married, and then realise they were wrong. <u>Not enough thinking comes into the relationship</u>, and the result is divorce.

Reason for breakdown.

Reason for breakdown but not developed.

Further reasons, but need development.

Q [b] ANSWER ONE – GRADE A

Overall religion is against divorce. <u>Many Christians believe that marriage is the uniting of two people through God, and that "no man must part what God has joined"</u> (as it says in Mark's Gospel). <u>In Christianity marriage is seen as a joining with God as well as with your partner, and it should last for a lifetime</u>. Many Christians teach that marriage is a holy joining by God, not just the priest. It is a sacrament, and by breaking the bond you are breaking your relationship with God.

Good reference to marriage and Christian teaching.

Marriage considered a life-long union.

Good understanding that marriage is a sacrament.

   If you get divorced you are <u>not allowed to remarry in many churches, as Christians believe that marriage is a life-long agreement</u>, and the only way it can be broken is if one person dies. Some churches, however, will give a blessing on a remarriage. <u>Catholics believe that marriage is for life but under special circumstances you are able to obtain an annulment</u>. <u>Cardinal Hume said, "divorce is a plague on society."</u> If divorce is to happen there must be a good reason e.g. one person has been unfaithful. <u>Other denominations may allow divorce but with sadness as the vows were made before God</u>.

Question of remarriage.

Catholic belief.

Good modern quote.

Diversity within Christianity.

Q [b] ANSWER TWO – GRADE C

Idea of marriage as a sacrament.

To some Christians <u>marriage is a sacrament</u>. To different <u>denominations</u> it has different interpretations. <u>Roman Catholics believe God</u> performs the ceremony through the priest. Hence divorce is harshly thought of by Catholics. <u>Protestants generally allow divorce although with sadness.</u> God intended people to get married. <u>The Bible teaches we should leave our mother and father, and find a person of the opposite sex.</u> It also teaches that a woman should not leave her husband, and he should not divorce his wife <u>unless there has been unfaithfulness.</u> Generally divorce is not encouraged, but not forbidden. There are, therefore, many reminders in the marriage ceremony of what marriage entails. <u>It is made clear that it is a life-long, monogamous state, and yet still divorce occurs.</u>

RC belief and Protestant views.

Biblical teaching.

Lacks biblical quotes and no discussion of vows.

Good reference to marriage as a life-long commitment.

Q [c] ANSWER ONE – GRADE A

I do agree with this statement as, <u>if God is joining you together with your partner, he should be the one to separate you</u>. Many religious people will argue that, just because their marriage has not worked out, it does not mean they are not still close to God. <u>Having a ceremony to end a marriage would allow the people involved to reaffirm their love for God.</u>

Good introduction.

Support for the idea.

Sometimes it is impossible to remain in a marriage e.g. if one person abuses the other. By <u>allowing God to break the bond the people involved are able to start again</u>.

Balanced argument.

On the other hand, people know what they are letting themselves in for when they get married, and if they believe strongly that God is joining them through marriage, they should not need a divorce ceremony, <u>as they should not need to end the marriage.</u> Some marriages do fail and <u>the couple might find it embarrassing</u> to have a ceremony in church to admit their failure. Perhaps <u>a compromise might be a secular ceremony</u> where the couple that is parting may not feel so threatened.

Importance of marriage discussed.

Idea of embarrassment.

Discussion of compromise.

Q [c] ANSWER TWO – GRADE C

<u>By having a religious ceremony to end a marriage, the church is condoning divorce</u>, and saying there is a place for it within Christianity. The marriage ceremony is a celebration of love. What is the divorce ceremony going to celebrate? However, as divorce is becoming a fact of life, <u>it is perhaps necessary to have a service to show others thinking of getting married how it should not be flippantly entered</u>, but I think this is unlikely. So much emphasis is placed on love, it is unlikely the church will accept a ceremony going against what they say.

Opposes statement.

Alternative view.

<u>Some might suggest a registry office ceremony but most couples separate with some bitterness and would probably not want to be reminded that their marriage has failed.</u>

Good conclusion.

Wealth and Poverty: What the Religions Say

BUDDHISM

"Wealth destroys the fool who seeks not the Beyond." [Dhammapada 345, 355]

"Of all gains, good health is the greatest. Of all wealth, contentment is the greatest." [Dhammapada 203: 5]

CHRISTIANITY

"No one can serve two masters . . . You cannot serve God and money." [Matthew 6: 24]

"The love of money is the root of all evils." [1 Timothy 6: 10]

"He who has two coats, let him share with him who has none; and he who has food, let him do likewise." [Luke 3: 11]

HINDUISM

"Let the rich man satisfy one who seeks help . . . For wealth revolves like the wheels of a chariot, coming now to one, now to another." [Rig Veda]

"The desire for wealth can never bring happiness." [Mahabharata]

ISLAM

"The righteous man is he . . . who for the love of Allah gives his wealth to his kinsfolk, to the orphans, to the needy, to the wayfarers and to the beggars, and for the redemption of captives." [Qur'an, 2: 177]

"On the day of judgement God Most High will say, 'Son of Adam, I was sick and you did not visit Me . . . Did you not know that My servant so-and-so was ill and yet you did not visit him? Did you not know that if you had visited him you soon would have found Me with him?'" [Hadith]

JUDAISM

"He who loves money will not be satisfied with money." [Ecclesiastes 5: 10]

"Blessed is he who considers the poor." [Psalm 41: 1]

"When the Holy One loves a man, He sends him a present in the shape of a poor man, so that he should perform some good deed to him, through the merit of which he may draw to himself a cord of grace." [Commentary on Genesis from the Holy Zohar]

SIKHISM

"Wealth, youth and flowers are short-lived as guests for four brief days." [Guru Granth Sahib 23]

"Each gives as much as he can spare and takes as much as he needs. Here there is no difference between kings and beggars." [Guru Amar Das]

"Blessed is the godly person and the riches they possess because they can be used for charitable purposes and to give happiness." [Guru Amar Das]

"A place in God's court can only be attained if we do service to others in this world." [Guru Granth Sahib 26]

1   What teachings about a correct attitude to wealth do the religions share? What would they say is an incorrect attitude to wealth?

2   Name three religious teachings which suggest that wealth should be shared with the poor. Why do you think the religions suggest this?

3   How would you answer the person who asked: Why doesn't God eliminate all poverty?

4   Do you think there would be fewer poor people in the world if religious people practised their religion more faithfully?

Islamic Relief

1   Study the information here about the organisation Islamic Relief. (It comes from an edition of the organisation's newspaper, *Partnership with the Needy*, published in the winter of 1998-99.) Write an account of the work of the organisation. Explain the religious principles which lie behind this work, by referring to the *Thinking Through Religion* student textbook (pages 60, 96-97, and 193).

For more information about the work of Islamic Relief, write to:
Islamic Relief,
Dept P12,
PO Box 13155,
London NW8 7WW

Kosovo – An Uncertain Future

$50,000 worth of aid being sent to Kosovo but funds urgently needed for winter clothing programme

Since late February 1998, Kosovo has been faced with an explosion of violence, resulting in the displacement of an estimated 400,000 people. The Serb army and police have systematically targeted the Albanian Muslim population in response to their call for greater independence from Serbia.

Islamic Relief has managed to finalise a winter clothing programme for displaced people in northern Kosovo. The overall emergency programme aims to cover a total of 50,000 displaced particularly vulnerable groups such as women, children, and the elderly, the majority of whom have fled their homes with only the bare essentials.

Palestinian Autonomous Area: Welcome Support for Two Educational Centres

Islamic Relief's Gaza office held the official opening of two Educational Enhancement Centres in November 1998. Both centres are located in refugee camps.

Pakistan – Free Eye Camps

One of the most precious gifts to humans is being able to see. One of the most common problems in developing countries is that of eye cataracts which gradually lead to blindness. A simple operation is all that's needed, but it is often not affordable to the poor.

As a response, Islamic Relief Pakistan has embarked on an ambitious programme through setting up short-term Eye Camps, particularly for the elderly. Each camp is provided "free of charge", and checks up to 7,000 patients during a one-week period.

Bangladesh Floods

In response to the worst flood to hit Bangladesh this century Islamic Relief has implemented the following programmes: Immediate Food and Essential Supplies.

To date Islamic Relief has distributed 30,000kg rice, 4,500kg pulses, 15,000kg potatoes, 3,300 water containers.

Total budget £31,500.

National Lottery Fever

National Lottery Fever

The introduction of the National Lottery into Britain in 1994 has brought untold misery to the lives of some, as well as material prosperity and happiness to others.

IN JUNE 1995 a man shot himself because he thought he had missed out on a two million pound lottery jackpot. Timothy O'Brien, 51, a father of two, had been sharing the cost of buying tickets with a friend. He shot himself in his attic when he realised that he had forgotten to buy tickets for the draw when his were the winning numbers.

Many people are concerned that the Lottery scratch cards are encouraging a highly addictive form of gambling. Scratch cards have been compared to fruit machines, because the small amounts of money people win now and then give them enough encouragement to keep playing. Habits are formed which are hard to stop. Branches of Gamblers Anonymous have been deluged with calls from people who feel they are scratch-card addicts. Some people, especially from poor areas, are spending all their housekeeping money on this new addiction, in the hope of finding a way out of their poverty. There has been a 17.5 per cent increase in calls to Gamblers Anonymous since the Lottery began.

So what do winners spend their money on? Those lucky ones tend to spend their winnings in similar ways. The largest proportion of the money is spent on their homes, followed by a holiday, a car, gifts to their children, a holiday home, boats and jewellery. However, not all winners splash out. At a recent dinner for 40 Lottery winners, we found that only half of these people had actually bought a new expensive house. Many had decided to stay where they were. For example, Doug Woods, 62, won £2,681,192 in September 1995. Since then he has given nearly half of it away to charities and friends, and has moved from his one-bedroom flat to a £66,000 two-bedroom bungalow 400 metres down the road. The idea that you have to buy a bigger and better house or car if you can afford it is a pretty narrow interpretation of the possible uses of money. The idea that material success can bring happiness is also a narrow view. It obviously doesn't in some cases.

Winning the Lottery is not necessarily the end to all problems. In some cases it's the start of new ones. Some lottery winners have spoken of their difficulties in coping with their wins. Mark Gardner, from Hastings, shared a 22 million-pound win. The press made his life a misery as it reported family arguments and alleged meanness. Other winners are besieged with demands for money, whilst some report how their relationships with other people change – for the worse. Gary Ashmore, 30, won £1,666,667 in June 1997. He is now considering returning to his job as a service adviser at a garage while trying a career in the music industry. At first he splashed out on high living – holidays and drink. He ended up having to go to a clinic for advice on alcohol abuse.

1 Why do people play the National Lottery? Do you think it is a form of gambling?

2 What image do you have of a Lottery winner?

3 Why does winning the Lottery not make all winners happy?

4 Many people give up their jobs when they win large sums of money. Do you think this is a wise thing to do?

5 What do you learn about the power of money from this article? Do you think winning large sums of money improves the quality of life?

Sample Examination Questions and Answers: Religion, Wealth and Poverty

Total for questions [a], [b], and [c]: 20 marks

[a] Describe five of the basic needs which many poor people in the world are lacking. [5 marks]

[b] Explain why religious people believe that they should help the poor. Refer to religious teachings in your answer. [10 marks]

[c] "If we all led simpler lives, we could help the poor and suffer less stress!"

How far do you agree with this comment? Give reasons to support your answer and show that you have thought about different points of view. [5 marks]

Q [a] ANSWER ONE – GRADE A

Many poor people are lacking <u>clean drinking water</u> to stop them from contracting illnesses. Often they have to travel miles to a water supply and then it isn't pure but contains many viruses. Also, good, <u>healthy food</u> is lacking in many poor countries and people suffer poor health from lack of protein and various vitamins.

Often they have <u>inadequate shelter</u>. Their homes do not protect them from the weather. They also lack power to heat and light their homes to prevent them catching illnesses in cold winters. Others have the problem of no air conditioning to keep them cool in hot climates.

They also lack immunisation to prevent them catching measles or polio or other horrible diseases. If they become ill there is inadequate <u>health care</u> and often only a few doctors. Medicines are also in short supply. In addition they lack <u>education</u> on how not to catch diseases and how to improve their circumstances.

Five basic needs are clearly identified, and each idea is developed and explained.

Q [a] ANSWER TWO – GRADE C

Poor people face many problems due to not having some of the most basic things:
<u>Food</u> Many people starve due to famine and insects eating crops, etc.
Money They have little money to buy basic tools, food, and construct <u>houses</u>. Often they live in a home made of corrugated iron.
<u>Clean water</u> Many poor people have dirty water to drink and have no supply of clean water – they can catch diseases and viruses more easily.
<u>Sanitation</u> Most poor people have no sewage system underground.

Four basic needs are mentioned, with some explanation showing the effects of their lack.

Q [b] ANSWER ONE – GRADE A

Some religious people have the same reasons for helping the poor as non-religious people do, for example because they feel guilty and unhappy that others are suffering while they are well and live in good conditions. This is often a <u>strong humanitarian motive</u> to help.

Reference to Old Testament teaching.

There are also specific religious reasons for religious people helping the poor. They believe that we are <u>all created by God, in His image (according to Genesis)</u> and so each person is precious. Also Jesus showed that Christians should <u>help the poor</u>. Jesus told stories such as the parables of the <u>Good Samaritan and the Sheep and Goats</u> which encourage helping others and this is a very important teaching for religious people such as the Red Cross to follow.

Muslims believe that <u>God/Allah sees all of what we do and do not do</u>. This is a strong reason why they believe they should help the poor as it will be seen by Allah and held up

Link to Judgement Day.

as <u>"evidence" on the Day of Judgement</u>. If they do not help someone in need, it will be held against them on the Day of Judgement and they may go to Hell (<u>jahannam</u>). As all Muslims strive to lead good lives to reach Paradise, they believe they must help the poor. It says in their scriptures <u>"He is not a believer who eats his fill while his neighbour stays hungry at his side."</u>

The moral conscience is seen to be a good motive.

Teaching of Jesus.

Reference to Allah being All-Knowing.

Good technical term.

Useful quote.

Good use of New Testament quote.

Jesus also taught about the Day of Judgement. He said, "It is much harder for a rich person to enter the Kingdom of God than for a camel to pass through the eye of a needle." This also shows the idea that Christians should help the poor and give their money to help the poor.

Muslims also may believe it as they fast to gain an understanding of the hardships the poor suffer and this may make them more willing to help. However, giving to the poor is also a part of Islamic teaching and faith – Muslims do it as it is one of the five Pillars of Islam, Zakat. This is a set proportion of their money which Muslims give each year to help the poor, and they do it as a part of their faith, without any other reason.

Action linked to Five Pillars.

Q [b] ANSWER TWO – GRADE C

Motive for action.

Religious people have to help the poor because they believe that they must share God's gifts with everyone including the poor. They, therefore, help the poor to fulfil God's wishes.

Christians believe that they must do this because of the teachings of the Bible. "It is much harder for a rich person to enter the Kingdom of God than it is for a camel to go through the eye of a needle." Christians believe that they must therefore give money to charity, etc. They try to follow the teaching of Jesus who taught that everyone is our neighbour and deserves our help e.g. in the story of the Good Samaritan. Muslims set aside an amount of money and give it for charity according to their religion. This is called Zakah.

Good biblical quote.

Reference to Jesus and his teaching.

Technical term.

Q [c] ANSWER ONE – GRADE A

Support for the statement

I agree up to a point. I agree that one can have too much wealth and a too complicated and busy life to have time to think about helping the poor. Stress is often caused by selfishness and greed and our constant rush trying to make money. I believe that everyone should live comfortably, and not have such a simple life that they are unhappy and suffer stress or illness. Lack of money can cause stress within marriages and families. Part of this is the demands of modern life and the wish to have expensive luxuries. In cases such as millionaires and lottery winners who have too much money to spend, it would not hurt for them to live simpler lives and make sure that some of the money goes to help the poor. I think that everyone should help and not be too materialistic, but as in Islam the donations should be proportioned to how wealthy a person is or else stress could be caused to those who are trying to help.

Need for money.

Technical term.

Alternative view.

Looking at it from another point of view, a simple life is not necessarily best because our current lifestyle creates wealth which could be used to help the poor. However, we could all live less complicated and stressful lives and help the poor as Jesus taught.

Q [c] ANSWER TWO – GRADE C

Recognises difference between theory and practice.

I agree with the statement up to a point because it works in theory like e.g. communism but in practice it often does not work exactly as planned. Some people are bound to be selfish and not want to lead simpler lives or help the poor. Also, if life was too simple there would be no planes to take support such as food to the poor, and so helping them would be difficult.

Opposes the statement.

Technical term and current lifestyle.

Lacks supporting religious teachings.

It is true that our modern lifestyle is very materialistic and stressful. There is no time to relax as everyone is so busy making money to buy things like TVs, washing machines, and computers. These used to be luxuries but now are regarded as a must, and so we work harder to get the money. This is stressful and the poor tend to get ignored because we haven't time for them as we have made money our god. I think that if we were satisfied with a little less and helped the poor it probably would help make life a little less stressful.

Reference to idolising money.

Personal opinion.

Colour is good, Lord

God, some people are saying that you are colour blind,
That you don't care whether a person is black or white,
Or any other colour,
And so we shouldn't care either.
Well, I can't accept that.
People are important!
Their eyes are important, their names are important,
Their race is important, and their colour is important.
Because white means something, black means something,
Yellow means something, and red means something.
Colour is good, Lord.
It's full of life.
Black people are good, white people are good,
Red people are good, and purple people are good.
There aren't many purple people around any more.
The people-eaters have almost destroyed them.
Lord, there won't be many black, brown, white, red,
Or yellow people, either,
If we let the people-eaters have their way,
And make us all a dirty grey.
We'll all be little robots or Xerox people,
Copied from some master copy
Prepared by a cold, calculating computer.
I have a hunch that Adam was black,
Eve was white, Cain was yellow,
And you were all the colours of the rainbow, then.
Lord, don't let me ever forget
The importance of every little difference
Between me and my brother,
Me and my parents, me and my maker,
And teach me to honour them just the way they are.
Then I'll be proud to be
The way you made me.

[Norman C. Habel, from Interrobang, Lutterworth Press,
1979]

1   Who do you think the "people-eaters" are?

2   Why does the author think colour is good?

3   Use the sentiments of this poem to explain why religions
    teach that prejudice and discrimination are wrong.

The Case of Stephen Lawrence

Macpherson Report challenges racist Britain

[25 February 1999]

Sir William Macpherson's report on the Metropolitan Police's handling of the investigation into the murder of black teenager Stephen Lawrence was published yesterday. The report describes the police as suffering from "institutional racism", and also criticises Britain's racist culture in general.

A-level student Stephen Lawrence was murdered in Eltham, southeast London, in April 1993. No one was convicted, although five white youths were heavily suspected.

The Macpherson Report refers to these "evil" white youths, saying that they had been "infected and invaded by gross and revolting racism".

Stephen's mother, Doreen Lawrence, said: "What I want to know is how my son bled to death while police officers stood by and watched. What was it that prevented police officers from giving my son first aid as he lay dying? No wonder that we are in the position we are today, that no one is serving time for the murder of my son. This society has stood by and allowed my son's killers to make a mockery of the law. The five boys lied under oath and the judge has chosen not to take any action against them."

Duwayne Brooks, who was with Stephen when he died, said: "Racism killed my friend Stephen."

Last night the Government recognised that "institutional racism" existed not only in the police force but in many organisations in British public life. It promised to fight racism wherever it is found. In future any organisation found guilty of racism could be prosecuted.

The Home Secretary said: "The very process of the Inquiry has opened all our eyes to what it is like to be black or Asian in Britain today . . . I want this report to be a watershed in our attitudes to racism."

Young people talk about their experiences of racism

"If a kid's parents are debating with their friends and they talk about 'big lips and chicken' stereotypes of black people, then the kids pick up on it and when they get to school they use the same thing. I've even had a teacher who cracked a racist joke about French people. I didn't laugh but everyone else did."
[Aminah Carter, 15]

"It's important to see colour but to respect it. We can live in peace but when you cuss what people believe in or their religion, you're stepping over the mark. Like when my mum's friend said, 'I don't like black people, but I like you.' You've got to be aware of the racism. There's certain things you don't say."
[Cariene Thomas-Bailey, 14]

"I've had several run-ins with the police. I was called 'nigger' by officers up in Richmond. I didn't feel anything. I was shocked. Another time, me and my cousin were stopped by two police officers. They asked us what our relationship was with each other. We said we were cousins. One said to the other, 'didn't you know they're all cousins?'"
[Jay Servin, 18]

"When you hear in the news about any trouble, it's always: 'he was a member of an Asian street gang'. A group of white people hanging out together doesn't constitute a gang but with blacks and Asians it does. When you're describing someone, a lot of people fail to mention that someone's white but they have to mention they're black."
[Mehrak Golestani, 15]

[Quotes from *The Guardian*, 25 February 1999]

What is institutional racism?

The Macpherson Report defines it as "the collective failure of an organisation to provide an appropriate and professional service to people because of their colour, culture, or ethnic origin. It can be seen or detected in processes, attitudes and behaviour which amount to discrimination through unwitting prejudice, ignorance, thoughtlessness and racist stereotyping which disadvantage minority ethnic people."

1 Make a list of all the different forms of racism spoken about by the young people quoted on the left. Add your own examples.

2 Describe briefly the details of the Macpherson inquiry into the police investigation of Stephen Lawrence's murder. How did Sir William Macpherson describe the suspect white youths? Why did the report criticise the police? What can we learn from this case?

3 Do you think society is infected with the disease of racism? Give reasons to support your argument.

Sample Examination Questions and Answers: Religion and Prejudice

Total for questions [a], [b], and [c]: 20 marks

[a] Describe five different causes of prejudice which might exist in a society that includes many different religions. [5 marks]

[b] Why would most religious people believe that they should not be prejudiced against other religious groups? Refer to religious teachings in your answer. [10 marks]

[c] "The teaching of Religious Education in schools is the best way to stop prejudice." How far do you agree with this statement? Give reasons to support your answer and show that you have thought about different points of view. [5 marks]

Q [a] ANSWER ONE – GRADE A

Five causes of prejudice are identified.

1 Racism is often the result of fear that people of other races will take jobs or take over the country.

2 Colour prejudice has come about because white people went out to Africa to "civilise the blacks" and they took them as slaves and treated them like animals. This prejudice has arisen out of ignorance and the belief that white people's customs and way of life are superior to others. Some newspapers and TV programmes have helped spread this type of prejudice. Parents can also cause their children to become prejudiced.

This is a detailed and explained account, and not just a list.

3 Comments about age such as you are too young or you lack experience or you are too old, although possibly true of some people, do not take into account the individual person.

4 Religious prejudice is the result of people believing that their denomination or religion is the one and only true way. The people in Northern Ireland have experienced these problems between Catholics and Protestants.

5 Men have often thought themselves superior to women because they are physically stronger and women have been stereotyped as people who stay at home and look after the children.

Q [a] ANSWER TWO – GRADE C

Four causes of prejudice are identified with some development and explanation.

1 Different races can cause prejudice – some people are discriminated against because of their colour e.g. black, white, Asian. This is often due to ignorance and misinformation about people of other races.

2 Different age groups – some people are victims of prejudice because people think they are too old or too young. This is often due to the fear of losing their employment. Fear of others is often the cause of prejudice.

3 Different Sex – Women especially can be the victims of prejudice although men can be too. Often women are stereotyped as those who stay at home and bring up the children.

No mention of religious prejudice.

4 Disabilities – Those who are in a wheelchair or are blind, deaf etc. can be discriminated against. These kinds of people can discriminate against those without disabilities too.

Q [b] ANSWER ONE – GRADE A

The golden rule of Christianity is to "love your neighbour as you love yourself", so this teaching suggests that most Christians should not be prejudiced against people of other faiths. Paul also said that "there is no difference between Jews and Gentiles, between slaves and free men, between men and women; you are all one in union

Useful scriptural references.

Gives examples of the teachings of Jesus, Paul and James.

with Christ Jesus." This implies that we should not be prejudiced. Also in the New Testament, James said that we should love everyone and Jesus did not appear prejudiced against Romans with their pagan gods. Christians recognise that God has given us freedom of choice and it is up to us how we respond to him. Some may find God a different way from other people, but they are entitled to their opinions.

Recognises that not all Christians always follow the teachings of their faith.

The answer is focused on the question.

It is true to say, however, that <u>some religious people, including Christians, have been prejudiced against those who have held different religious beliefs e.g. the Roman Catholics and Protestants in Northern Ireland, the Crusaders and the Spanish Armada.</u> Most Christians would say that these are examples where Christians have not followed the teachings of Jesus to love everyone, including our enemies.

Q [b] ANSWER TWO – GRADE C

General point included.

Most religious people have been taught to love everybody because they are equal. Christians are taught to "<u>love thy neighbour</u>" and to <u>treat others as they would want to be treated themselves.</u> Christians believe in freedom of choice so they understand that others have <u>the right to believe what they want.</u> Even if religions do not agree with one another, they are taught to love one another and not cause prejudice or suffering or evil. For example, <u>Jesus helped non-Jews, e.g. he healed a Samaritan leper.</u> Paul teaches "<u>There is neither man nor woman, Jew nor gentile – all are equal in the eyes of Jesus.</u>" Prejudice causes suffering and evil and religious people are taught that evil is a sin so if they are prejudiced they are sinning and this is not right.

Good scriptural references.

Gives example of Jesus helping a Gentile.

Q [c] ANSWER ONE – GRADE A

R.E. is one method of stopping prejudice. <u>One of the main causes is ignorance and any education to overcome that must be good.</u> Also in R.E. there may be <u>the opportunity to discuss prejudice among pupils of different nationalities or religions who are present in the class. Fears and misunderstandings can be brought out into the open and dealt with. Prejudices which have arisen at home can be shown to be unfounded.</u>

Good discussion of the contribution RE can make.

Explores the value of other ways.

But R.E. is not the only place where prejudice can be stopped. <u>Laws can help and books and newspapers can have a big influence.</u> It is <u>important for churches to tell their congregations that Jesus taught that we should not be prejudiced. We are all made in the image of God.</u> Parents also have a big responsibility to bring up their children not to hold prejudices.

Brings in religious ideas.

Good example.

Is R.E. the best way? I think it is <u>an important way but one of many.</u> If we want a society like <u>Martin Luther King</u> said in his famous "dream" speech, then we need to use every method possible, and <u>R.E. lessons can definitely be effective if the teacher is not prejudiced.</u>

Comes to a reasoned conclusion.

Q [c] ANSWER TWO – GRADE C

Two valid points in favour of the statement.

I think R.E. is a good idea because <u>it does help to stop prejudice because people learn about different people's points of view</u> and learn not to be prejudiced. Also, it is <u>easier to stop prejudice when people are young because they are more prepared to listen and learn.</u> However, <u>the best way is for parents to stop prejudice</u> when their children are young. Children are even more likely to listen to their parents and do as they are told and it will set a firm foundation for the rest of their lives. Also, <u>television and the media can be used to influence people and help to remove the fear and ignorance which cause prejudice.</u>

Counter-arguments.

Lacks reference to a religious teaching which would support the arguments.

Personal opinion.

So <u>I see R.E. as one tool among many of helping get rid of prejudice but not necessarily the best.</u>

Religion in Action

Chapters 17, 18, and 19 encourage students to explore:

Work and leisure

▸ The reasons why people value work and leisure
▸ Values promoted in the work place
▸ The spiritual quality of work and leisure
▸ Work and business ethics
▸ Religious responses to certain forms of work
▸ Work as vocation

Religion and Science

▸ The historical debate between Science and Religion
▸ Origins of the universe – cosmology; arguments from accident or design (see also Chapter 13)
▸ Origins of life – creation and evolution
▸ Different types of knowing and knowledge (e.g. knowledge of faith and scientific knowledge)
▸ The nature of miracles
▸ The way in which science challenges some religious positions

Religion, the arts, and the media

▸ The ability of the arts to express religious ideas and beliefs
▸ The variety and range of specifically religious programmes on radio and television
▸ The way religious and moral issues are dealt with in the media
▸ The values and beliefs expressed through the media, especially television and the internet
▸ Potential dangers of the media

SEG coursework

For the SEG examination, students may choose to offer coursework on "Religion in Action". Six of the broad subject areas within which this coursework should fit are covered in chapters 14-19 of *Thinking Through Religion* (Religion and Relationships; Religion, Wealth and Poverty; Religion and Prejudice; Religion, Work and Leisure; Religion and Science; Religion and the Media and Arts). Study Skills Sheets 17. 3, 17. 4, 18. 1, 18. 2, 19. 3, and 19. 4 show examples of SEG coursework with examiners' comments.

Examination candidates are expected to:

▸ demonstrate knowledge and understanding of the chosen topic;
▸ show understanding of the teachings of the religion(s) studied, recognising and explaining differences within the tradition(s) where appropriate;
▸ demonstrate how sacred texts, religious principles, and statements by religious authorities are applied to issues;
▸ show they have considered the links between religion and action in the lives of believers;
▸ present an "holistic" response which allows the religion as a whole to be glimpsed in its response to a single issue;
▸ use relevant technical language precisely throughout;
▸ show they have considered and evaluated in depth their own responses to the subject being studied, by using a range of reasoned arguments.

Activity Sheet/Study Skills Sheet	Key concept for students to consider
17.1 The Body Shop	The nature of work and its contribution to human fulfilment.
17.2 A Million Pound Lesson	How work not only earns a wage but also can contribute to society.
17.3 Sample Coursework*	Sample coursework on the balance between work and leisure.
17.4 Sample Coursework*	Sample coursework on Sunday as a day of rest.
18.1 Sample Coursework*	Sample coursework on the importance of the miraculous.
18.2 Sample Coursework*	Sample coursework on the place of miracles in the scientific age.
19.1 Trained to Kill: Violence in the Media	The effect that violence in the media can have on people.
19.2 and **19.3** Sample Coursework*	Sample coursework on the arts and worship.
19.4 Sample Coursework*	Sample coursework on making a religious television programme.
20 Has the Human Race Progressed?	As technology progresses, have human beings become more or less moral?

* See notes about SEG coursework on page 125.

The Body Shop

"All staff at The Body Shop are allowed paid time off, half a day per month, to take part in a community project of their choice. Whether caring for locally disadvantaged people, cleaning up the local environment or working with sick animals, staff can feel connected and uplifted. It is another of those not so secret ingredients that help our staff raise their sense of self.

"Let me share another example with you. In 1990, shocked by the news coverage of the legacies of Nicolae Ceausescu's 26 years of dictatorship in Romania, I went out myself to see how we could help. I was horrified by what I saw. The horror filled my thoughts for weeks. But within just six weeks, we'd set up the Romanian Relief Drive. Staff clamoured to be among the volunteers to go out there and help refurbish the orphanages, hold babies with AIDS and give them something many had never had before – love and care.

"Now called the Eastern Europe Relief Drive, the programme is still run on next to nothing, by a handful of young staff members. Their desire to help out has been shared by over 450 members of our staff from around the world who have been out to work as volunteers. The staff come back changed people. Their values suddenly take a leap into a previously unknown source of power for them. They start dreaming of noble purposes."

[Anita Roddick, founder of the Body Shop, quoted in Jack Canfield and Jacqueline Miller, *Heart at Work: Stories and Strategies for building self-esteem and reawakening the soul at work*, McGraw Hill, 1996]

1 In groups, collect reasons why you think people go to work. Is it just to earn money or can work also give them some spiritual benefit?

2 Study the account of Anita Roddick's Body Shop organisation and consider how she would answer question 1.

3 (a) Why do you think Anita Roddick, founder of the Body Shop, gives all her employees a half day per month off work to take part in community projects? What lessons is she trying to teach?
(b) If you were to work for the Body Shop, what community project would you like to take part in? Explain why.

A Million Pound Lesson

The other year when I was travelling I learned a £1 million lesson from a taxi driver. The ride itself cost me only £8.

I had arrived by train in London for a meeting. It was a flying visit. I didn t intend to stop long. As I left the station a spotless taxi pulled up. Before I could say anything the driver had got out and opened the passenger door for me to climb in. I had never had such service before. The driver made sure that I was comfortably seated before he closed the door and got into the front seat. Before he started to drive off he mentioned that the neatly folded newspaper placed beside me was for my use. He then asked whether I would like music played and, if so, what sort? The driver had a whole range of tapes in the cab.

I could not believe the service I was receiving. I couldn t help but say to him, I notice that you take great pride in your work. I bet you have quite a story to tell.

He explained that for many years of his life he had worked as a well-paid businessman in the City. In fact, he had earned over £1 million a year. He could afford to buy whatever he wanted. One day, however, he realised that he was no longer enjoying his job. He felt as though he was in a rat race and couldn t escape from it. Life had lost its quality value. He made a decision to do something that he would enjoy doing for the rest of his life. He loved cars and loved meeting people. He had always had a secret desire to be a cab driver. Not a regular taxi driver, but a truly professional one.

One thing I know for sure, he said. To be *good* in my business I could simply just meet the expectations of my passengers. But to be *great* in my business, I have to exceed the customer s expectations!

He had therefore set out to be a *great* cab driver.

Did I tip him big time? You bet!

Q

1 What sort of service do you think the passenger expected when he got into the taxi? How was he surprised?

2 Why do you think the taxi driver took such pride in his work? In what sense does his work have a "spiritual quality"?

3 What does this true story teach us about the nature of work?

Sample Coursework

Discuss the teachings and views of one religion about the balance which should exist between work and leisure in the life of each person.

The Teachings and Views of Christianity on the Balance between Work and Leisure

Most Christians have decided there is a place for both work and leisure in life. After all, Paul said that those who refused to work should not be allowed to eat, but Jesus showed that leisure is equally important as he used to go away to the hills to be alone and rest and pray. You cannot work all the time as you need time to relax and have fun. Christians, however, teach that it is important to use your talents in order to obtain the basic necessities of life such as food, shelter and clothing or to fulfil your vocation in life. Vocations may be jobs such as teaching, nursing or any of the caring professions. Any job could be a vocation if you believed that God had particularly called you to do it.

In his letters, Paul suggests that it is right to do something constructive for society. You may say but what about monks and nuns? Haven't monks and nuns given up normal work and wealth in order to devote their whole lives to meditation and prayer? Yes, that is true, but they have continued to work. In many instances they may have a farm attached to the monastery, as in the case of Buckfastleigh. However, their work hasn't just been going out to work and earning money in the usual sense, as they have wished to devote their lives to following God and this might involve, for example, a lot of prayer. They haven't just become lazy.

A good example of someone who showed this was Mother Teresa. With the Sisters of Charity she helped the poor and destitute in India as her calling from God. She went to India, first as a nun and teacher and then she believed that God was asking her to do more. She began teaching in the worst slums in Calcutta and saw the children and adults dying in a filthy and uncared-for state. She couldn't stand by and just watch. She had to care for the dying and the abandoned orphans. Eating the simplest food and having no money of her own, she relied upon others to fund her and the Sisters who joined her. Now they run hospitals for lepers and do what they can to feed and care for the hungry and diseased. Mother Teresa found inspiration in the teaching of Jesus in the Parable of the Sheep and Goats. She wanted to help. That was her work and vocation in life and she is an inspiration to thousands of Christians in the world.

On the other hand, Christians regard Sunday as God's day, a day of rest and worship. Although the scriptures say that God rested on the seventh day and in the Ten Commandments it says that the Sabbath Day, the Saturday, should be kept holy, Christians have changed this to the first day of the week. This is because Jesus rose from the dead on the Sunday, the Holy Spirit came at Pentecost (a Sunday) and they want to put God first in their lives. So Christians have been prepared to work for up to six days a week but many have campaigned to keep Sunday special. Some, however, have recognised that some jobs are essential whatever day of the week it is and they have realised that Jesus healed the sick, for example, on the Sabbath.

In conclusion I would say that many Christians have fulfilled their vocation in life as they believe that God has a plan, will and purpose for everyone's life. Most have seen work as an opportunity to use their talents and have worked to the best of their ability in order to make a positive and useful contribution to society. Voluntary work has been carried out by many Christians, working for charities or generally making a positive contribution to society. All of this has generally been seen within the context of needing to spend time with the family and keeping Sunday special as a day of rest and worship. Christians recognise that there is a need to spend quality time with the family. This you cannot do if you are always working. So the Christian faith teaches that there is an important role for both work and leisure time and that it is important not to neglect one for the other.

Examiner's comment:

This is a Grade A answer because:

▶ it includes good scriptural references as a basis for Christian belief and action, e.g. teaching of Jesus and Paul;

▶ it gives good examples of how and why Christians spend their work and leisure time as they do, e.g. charity work, Sundays;

▶ it is focused on the question and doesn't include a lot of irrelevant material;

▶ technical terms such as vocation and the Sabbath are used appropriately.

However,

▶ the evidence could be used more effectively in answering the question concerning what the balance should be between work and leisure.

Sample Coursework

Does it matter that Sunday is no longer recognised as a national "day of rest"?

Should Sunday be a "day of rest"?

Nowadays many people have to work on Sundays. There are so many jobs to be done seven days a week. It may be nice to have the day off but farmers need to look after their cattle, milk the cows etc. every day of the week. Patients in hospital need looking after as well. It isn't as simple as Sunday should be kept as a national "day of rest". Also, people are demanding more and more on a Sunday. They don't want to just stay at home and get bored. They want to shop or have entertainment. It is a family day for many and they want to go out for a meal or to do some leisure activities or some shopping. Probably fewer people go to church on a Sunday these days than earlier this century and so they want more to do. They don't want to just stay in and watch the television all the time.

Others like the idea of having a weekend job to earn a little money. Students can get jobs like waitressing or serving in a shop. Double time is often paid on a Sunday so it is good pay. To stop people getting this would not be a very popular move and anyway does it matter if Sunday is not kept as a national "day of rest"?

Well, Christians in particular see Sunday as a very special day. Although originally the Sabbath was from Friday evening to Saturday evening, Christians celebrate the resurrection of Jesus on the first day of the week. They, therefore, want to be able to attend church and worship God without having to work. To them, Sunday should be special and many want Sunday as a national "day of rest".

It is also a good thing to have a day without the pressures of work and be able to spend it relaxing with the family. If Sunday became just another day of the week, this might not be possible. So others apart from Christians also value a rest day. Some, however, do have other days of the week as rest days, e.g. the Jews and Saturday.

I think that it is important for everyone to be able to have freedom of choice. If they wish to work on Sunday, that's up to them. If they wish to spend the day worshipping God they should be allowed to do so. What I am against is one group imposing their opinions on others. Should we keep Sunday special? On balance I would like it to be different from other days of the week. I wouldn't want to have to go to school on a Sunday for example and I enjoy spending it with my family and friends. So yes, I think it should be different from a week day when people are free to worship God and do other things that they enjoy. To insist that Sunday should be kept as a national "day of rest" is, however, a little dangerous because it is infringing on the rights of others who perhaps have another day as their holy day, e.g. the Muslims and Friday. To many Christians, however, it is obviously a thing to regret that Sunday is no longer recognised as a national "day of rest" to the same degree as it was years ago when more people attended church and shops stayed shut.

Examiner's comment:
This is a Grade A answer because:

- it comes to a reasoned conclusion and makes appropriate points concerning freedom of choice;
- it includes well-supported arguments;
- it is balanced in its approach and deals with the issue sensitively, recognising the differences which exist and the reasons for them.

Sample Coursework

Using the religion you have studied, explain the importance of the miraculous to believers.

The Importance of the Miraculous for Christians

The Christian faith is based on the miraculous . . . that God spoke the universe into existence, that sin entered the world and corrupted it but God in his grace and mercy miraculously sent his only son to be the atonement and redeem the world and to bring wholeness and healing.

Jesus' life is surrounded by the miraculous. The prophets said he would be born as a descendant of King David in Bethlehem, preach in parables, heal the sick, be put to death and rise again. Over three hundred prophecies, written hundreds of years before his birth, came true in Jesus. Jesus came from a virgin birth, angels appeared praising God, people were given messages from God either by angels or in dreams or visions, and a new star appeared. You cannot get much more miraculous than that!

At Jesus' baptism God spoke. Later Jesus performed healing and forgiveness miracles, exorcisms (casting out of evil spirits), nature miracles and raising people from the dead. At the transfiguration his physical appearance became dazzling white as he appeared with Moses (the Law giver) and Elijah (the prophet). The gospels finish with the resurrection from the dead and the ascension into heaven, and the promise that Jesus would return.

If you believe all of this you are way outside the realms of science and into the miraculous in a big way. E. H. Andrews said, "The miraculous is absolutely basic to Christianity." The supernatural and miraculous have to be important to believers or else so much of the religion is wiped out and completely lost. Would there be a religion at all?

Some Christians would say that there would. They are not so much into the miraculous side of the religion. This group is often known as the "Liberals". To this group the teaching of Jesus about love, peace and social justice is the most important element of the gospel. The former Bishop of Durham, Dr. David Jenkins, questioned whether or not Jesus was really born of a virgin, or physically rose from the dead, but still he believed in the basic teaching of Jesus as the right moral code by which we should all strive to live.

The Liberals do not accept all the teaching in the Bible as necessarily literally the truth. They see the miracle stories of Jesus as having important symbolic meaning and say that perhaps there is a scientific explanation for the so-called miracle. A good example of this is the story of the feeding of the 5,000. They might argue that if a small boy had his picnic lunch with him, others probably did as well. So after Jesus had said grace, everyone opened up their picnics and shared them around. So all the people were fed. More importantly they would argue that Jesus fed the people spiritually and he is able to also do this for us. If there was a miracle, it was that Jesus taught them to share with each other.

To other Christians the miraculous is absolutely vital and is the centre of their belief and action. They may be known as fundamentalists or conservatives in terms of their theology and their position is summed up by William S. Plumer when he wrote, "A religion without wonders is false. A theology without wonders is heretical."

The early Christians not only believed in the miracles of Jesus but they expected miracles to happen. John wrote, "In his disciples' presence Jesus performed many other miracles which are not written down in this book. But these have been written in order that you may believe that Jesus is the Messiah, the Son of God, and that through your faith in him you may have life." (John 20: 30-31). The early Christians prayed for miracles. In Acts it says that prison doors burst open and Peter was released, a lame man is healed outside the temple, Tabitha is brought back from the dead and "Many miracles and wonders were being done through the apostles, and everyone was filled with awe." (Acts 2: 43). So important were these miracles, including the belief that Jesus was the Messiah and had risen from the dead, that the early Christians were able to withstand terrible persecution and still stick to their beliefs. It inspired them to preach the gospel despite witnessing the deaths of friends and loved ones, and the knowledge that they too might be beaten, or killed.

The miraculous faith was so important that it inspired writers to record the events and so the New Testament was written. Since then many have given their lives to spread the good news and translate the Bible into different languages so that people are able to read it. No opposition, however hostile, has been able to crush it.

Today Christians are influenced by their belief in the miraculous to pray for the sick and enjoy the mystery of the Eucharist. Roman Catholics believe in transubstantiation where, after dedication, the bread and wine miraculously become the body and blood of Jesus. Taking the host is the very centre of their Christian worship as the presence of the living Jesus is very real to them. Christians worship a risen, glorified Jesus – if that isn't miraculous, what is? Their whole religion and practice of their faith are based on the miraculous.

Some Christians hold special healing services for those who are unwell. Some even anoint the sick with oil. Some have prayers for healing at Holy Communion. Some just pray for those who need help and that God will change circumstances when they say their daily prayers. To me that is just a small part of the belief in the supernatural. The whole of Christianity is based on the supernatural both in this life and the belief in the next. Christians hope, trust and believe that miraculously we shall rise again from the dead and through the saving grace of Jesus have life with God in heaven for all eternity. Can anything be more important than that?

Examiner's comment:

This is a Grade A answer because:

- it shows complex understanding of the issues and draws on a wide range of sources;
- it includes good quotes from the Bible and contemporary Christians;
- technical language is used precisely throughout, e.g. transubstantiation, Eucharist;
- it includes differences in belief within Christianity regarding the miraculous;
- it includes not only belief but also actions because of what is believed;
- it is an "holistic" response and does not just concentrate on one aspect of miraculous belief and action;
- it is clearly focused on the question.

Sample Coursework

"Miracles have no place in the modern scientific age." How far do you agree?

"Miracles have no place in the modern scientific age"

The Oxford Dictionary defines a miracle as "a remarkable and welcome event that seems impossible to explain by the laws of nature and is therefore attributed to a supernatural agency." Perhaps in today's world we are tempted to think that science has all the answers. It is true that scientists have made marvellous advances in discoveries concerning medicine such as penicillin and other drugs. They have looked at the moon and planets by sending rockets and probes to many parts of the solar system. They have explored the depths of the ocean, split the atom and invented machines for numerous things, but still there are mysteries to be solved. Theories have been put forward to explain the state of the universe and advances in knowledge have been so great that it is tempting to say that "Miracles have no place in the modern scientific age".

Many events that have been credited as miraculous may well have rational scientific explanations. 2,000 years ago people's medical science was nowhere near as advanced as ours today. If we were able to take our knowledge back to the time of Jesus it may be possible to explain many of the so-called miracles. For example, was Jairus' daughter in a coma and just at the moment when Jesus took her by the hand did she recover? Did a weather front pass over just as Jesus woke from his sleep and as he spoke to the storm on Lake Galilee?

On the other hand, we are still searching for answers to make sense of many events that happen. Our knowledge of the universe is still relatively small. There is so much that we still do not know. If Jesus is the "word" and spoke the universe into existence, this makes healing a leper or blind man or someone who is suffering from cancer rather a small matter in comparison.

On the other hand, many believe that the stories in the gospels were exaggerated as they were written by supporters of Jesus. They wanted people to be impressed by him and so follow him. They wished people to believe that he was the son of God and so wanted to make him look impressive. This does not explain, however, why Josephus, a Jewish historian who wasn't a Christian, regarded Jesus as a miracle worker or at the least a sorceror. Perhaps that is what he was? Perhaps he used hypnotism to get people either to believe that they were healed or to believe that a miracle had taken place. But that doesn't explain why people believe in miracles today.

I believe that miracles might happen because I have met people who have claimed to have been healed in the name of Jesus Christ. I accept, however, that they could have got it wrong and their healing could have a scientific explanation. Throughout history, however, in all sorts of cultures and religions, there have been incidents which have been claimed to have been miracles. For example, a couple of years ago it is claimed that statues in Hindu Temples in various parts of the world started drinking milk, including a temple in London. In the Old Testament there is the story of Moses parting the Red Sea, of God feeding the Children of Israel with manna from heaven, and of Elisha healing Naaman the Syrian leper and of many other miraculous events.

So to say that miracles have no place in the modern scientific age is a very dismissive statement. There are too many situations past and present that appear to be true for me just to dismiss miracles as made up nonsense.

Examiner's comment:
This is a Grade A answer because:

▸ the evidence has been used appropriately and the arguments developed logically;
▸ it recognises the possible tensions between religious believers and scientists;
▸ it clearly focuses on answering the question;
▸ the arguments are well supported with appropriate evidence;

▸ it gives arguments for and against and has a reasoned conclusion.

However,

▸ it fails to include the fact that many scientists believe in the miraculous.

Trained to Kill: Violence in the Media

In 1993 one story above others hit the headlines: the killing of two-year-old James Bulger by two ten-year-olds. But this was not an isolated incident. During the 1990s there was an increase in violent crime amongst the young. From where do young people get these violent ideas?

1   Do you watch violent films or play with video and computer games which contain violence? If so, why do you do this? What effect do you think violence on TV has? Do you think it encourages young people to become violent?

TRAINING KIDS TO KILL

David Grossman is a military expert on the psychology of killing. He believes that the media are training kids to kill .

 Killing requires training because there is an in-built aversion to killing one s own kind. It does not come naturally. You have to be taught to kill. Children don t naturally kill; they learn it from violence in the home, and most pervasively, from violence as entertainment in television, movies, and interactive games.
[quoted in *Christianity Today*, 10 August 1998]

Grossman believes that television, films, and computer games teach young people to become more violent in the following three ways:

1. They desensitise children to violence. Children watch television from an early age. They gradually become desensitised to all the violence they see: it no longer shocks them and they see it as normal.

2. They condition children to derive pleasure from violence. As children see more and more television violence, they cease to be horrified by it. Instead, they associate such films with pleasure and carry on eating their popcorn and drinking pop!

 We have raised a generation of barbarians who have learned to associate violence with pleasure. The result is a phenomenon that functions much like AIDS, which I call AVIDS — Acquired Violence Immune Deficiency Syndrome. AIDS has never killed anybody. It destroys your immune system, and then other diseases that shouldn t kill you become fatal. Television violence by itself does not kill you. It destroys your violence immune system and conditions you to derive pleasure from violence.

3. They train children to be violent as a reflex action. Grossman calls this operant conditioning : it s as if children are programmed always to react in a certain way, without needing to think. In the army soldiers are trained to shoot as soon as they see the enemy. So with the video and computer games that children play: children learn to shoot the enemy as a reflex reaction. The games lead the children to develop violent habits.

Fifteen years after the introduction of TV, homicides, rapes and assaults doubled in the United States. [American Medical Association]

Few researchers bother any longer to dispute that bloodshed on TV and in the movies has an effect on kids who witness it.

THE FIFTEEN YEAR RULE

The Journal of the American Medical Association has published evidence of what happens to a society once the TV, and TV violence, is introduced:

 In every nation, region, or city with television, there is an immediate explosion of violence on the playground, and within 15 years there is a doubling of the murder rate. Why 15 years? That is how long it takes for the brutalisation of a three-to-five year-old to reach the prime crime age . Today the data linking violence in the media to violence in society are superior to those linking cancer and tobacco. Hundreds of sound scientific studies demonstrate the social impact of brutalisation by the media.

2   When you watch TV this week monitor the amount of violence you see. It could be on news programmes and documentaries as well as in fictional programmes and films. Notice domestic violence as well as national and international violence.

3   "The average child gets more one-to-one communication from TV than from all her parents and teachers combined." Do you agree? What impact do you think the TV has?

4   What can be done to combat all the TV violence? Should there be laws against TV violence? Are TV producers acting responsibly? If you had children, would you censor what they watch on TV? Is this practical or realistic?

Sample Coursework

Select one religion you have studied and discuss how the arts can be used to enrich worship.

The Arts in Christian Worship

Many Christian denominations have made great use of the Arts to enrich their worship. Paintings, sculptures, poetry, drama, music, dance, writings and stained glass windows have all been used to present religious ideas and add to worship. On entering some churches it would be difficult not to be affected by the atmosphere and beauty created by gifted artists wishing to glorify God. In Eastern Orthodox churches the sense of the mystery and awe and wonder of God is enhanced by the iconostasis. This screen, which separates the priest in the sanctuary from the congregation in the nave, is covered with colourful icons depicting biblical scenes or saints. Many Roman Catholic and Anglican churches are also very ornate in their decoration. Statues of Mary or the crucifix may form part of the focus of worship and encourage worshippers to centre their thoughts on Jesus, the incarnation and the sacrifice he made on our behalf at the crucifixion.

Stained glass windows, beautifully and colourfully made, remind worshippers of a particular religious theme. The focus point in Chulmleigh Parish Church is the ascension of Jesus. Various windows tell his life story from the nativity, through the baptism, preaching, healing the sick, showing his love for children, to the death and resurrection and then finally his rising to heaven. As the congregation face the altar they see the picture of Jesus high above the people and this may act as a focal point and aid to worship.

In other churches a sagging figure of Jesus hanging on a cross may be central to the eyeline. The crucifix portrays the image of Jesus being the atonement for sin, the saviour and redeemer of the world. The cost of that sacrifice made on behalf of all is evident to see and the worshipper is reminded to ask forgiveness and say thank you for Jesus' love.

One other stained glass window in Chulmleigh Church shows a group of angels playing a variety of musical instruments. Music plays a major role in most Christian worship, whether in charismatic churches or more traditional ones. In many it is the Church organist who plays the music for the songs and hymns but increasingly groups of musicians are being formed with keyboards, guitars, drums, flutes etc. being used. Often there is a worship leader who attempts to lead the congregation in song so that they become "lost in wonder and praise". Music is a powerful medium which Christians believe can lead people into the presence of God. All kinds of emotions can be touched and different atmospheres created. Songs and music may be used to express love for Jesus, or the tempo can be changed dramatically into a Christian battle song and song of victory and triumph, e.g. "The Battle belongs to the Lord."

Great hymn writers have tried to capture the meaning of the Christian faith in their words. Charles Wesley, Isaac Watts, Sankey and Moody and more recently Graham Kendrick have written words and music which provide a way of expressing praise, thanksgiving, and adoration.

Sometimes singing may be accompanied by dance. The dancer may use the dance art form to express their interpretation of the meaning of the song. Occasionally ribbons or flags may also be used. This adds to the spectacle and attractiveness of the occasion and may be ideal for family services.

Drama also forms part of many services which include young people. Perhaps instead of just reading a passage from the Bible, the story will be acted out and so it becomes more visual and perhaps more meaningful to the worshippers. Dramatic readings may also help to liven up the worship.

There is no doubt that the various art forms can be used to add colour, atmosphere, teaching, mystery, awe, emotion, variety, action and much more to worship. Used correctly, some of these art forms can inspire worshippers to focus fully and reach great heights of worship as they try to give God the glory due to him.

Examiner's comment:
This is a Grade A answer because:
▶ it includes relevant material from a wide variety of areas/sources;
▶ it shows sophisticated understanding of a range of ways in which the arts are used to enhance worship;
▶ it is an "holistic" response, revealing an understanding of the Christian religion through its focused coverage of paintings, sculptures, poetry, drama, music, dance, writings and stained glass windows;
▶ it includes technical language, e.g. iconostasis, sanctuary and nave;
▶ differences between various denominations are included and explained;
▶ there is a clear link between religion and action;
▶ it shows evidence of analysing how the Arts contribute to worship.

Sample Coursework

Do the Arts enhance religious belief or are they a distraction?

The Pros and Cons of the Arts for Religious Believers

Not all Christians enjoy noisy services which are jam-packed full of action. They may not even like beautiful decorated churches with ornate statues, colourful stained glass windows etc. To them, the expression of the different artists are not a help to worship or an aid to religious belief but rather a distraction. They are far happier in a plain quiet room where they can wait for God to speak to them through the Holy Spirit. There they can concentrate without fear of focusing upon a beautiful painting or being distracted by something else that is going on. The Society of Friends, for example, as they meet in a Quaker meeting house, wait for God to move. Aids to worship are not necessary to them.

Many other Christians would find a Quaker meeting strange and uninspiring. They prefer lively music with drums, guitars and keyboard. Particularly young people like plenty of action so that they don't get bored. Having to sit for long periods of time and listen to a lengthy sermon which they probably don't understand is not for them.

Entering a beautiful church can be inspiring and uplifting and this feeling can be further enhanced by using different art forms to portray the message of the gospel. Using different art forms can lead to greater participation by the congregation but can also be very effective in getting over the Christian message. Handel's Messiah or a great hymn like "When I survey the wondrous cross" can take you to the very heart of the Christian message. Stained glass windows can remind you of an important Christian story. It was for this purpose that many of them were made in the Middle Ages when few people could read the Bible for themselves.

Of course, there is a danger that people can worship the crucifix rather than the risen Jesus. People can get so excited with the music that they forget who they are worshipping, or they could get so enthusiastic about a painting or picture that they miss what is really happening in the service.

I think that what works for one person might not for another. For some, a particular art form may indeed lead them into real worship. For others it may be a total distraction and very annoying. Perhaps it is for this very reason that we have so many different types of churches, each hopefully providing what its individual congregation needs.

Examiner's comment:

This is a Grade A answer because:

▶ it gives well-supported arguments both for and against;
▶ it recognises the complexity of the issue in that there are tensions and differences of opinion between worshippers over the use of the Arts in worship;
▶ it comes to a reasoned conclusion;
▶ it is clearly focused on answering the question.

Sample Coursework

(a) Devise a TV programme that will portray the life of a religion in Britain today. Assume that it is being made on behalf of this religion; and that the aim of the programme is to show the religion's best points.

A TV Programme on Christianity

The religion I have chosen to portray is Christianity in Britain Today.

The programme would open with shots of praise and worship at "Spring Harvest", Minehead. The camera will focus first on the congregation singing a lively praise song such as "Come on and celebrate" or "Praise Him on the trumpet, the psaltery and harp". Individuals who are dancing or raising their hands in the air and looking as though they are really enjoying themselves would form the centre of the pictures. Then the camera will zoom in towards the music band on stage with guitars, drums, flutes and other musical instruments and those who are leading the singing. Also on stage would be a dancer who is interpreting the words and music. The whole of this first part of the introduction would be aimed at attracting the attention of the viewer by presenting a lively image of Christians having a fun time praising the Lord. The people shown will be mainly people under forty and include many teenagers.

All of these opening shots would be aimed at helping to overcome the image that Christianity is boring and just for old people. The commentator would then welcome viewers and invite them to see what Christianity is all about. The mood would then change as the commentator's voice fades and is replaced by a worship song e.g. "Abba Father, let me be Yours and Yours alone". After this love song to Jesus, the commentator would explain that Christians believe that Jesus is the Son of God and came to this earth to bring salvation and redeem us from our sin. This message would be reinforced by a soloist singing (accompanied by the music group) the following song and by the words appearing at the bottom of the screen:

"You laid aside Your majesty,
gave up everything for me,
suffered at the hands of those You had created;
You took all my guilt and shame,
when You died and rose again;
now today You reign in heaven and earth exalted,
I really want to worship You, My Lord,
You have won my heart and I am Yours for ever and ever;
I will love You,
You are the only one who died for me,
gave Your life to set me free,
so I lift my voice to You in adoration."

Then as the congregation stands and repeats this song together in the background, a well-known Christian (e.g. someone from Christians in Sport or Cliff Richard) explains the Christian belief concerning the love and grace of the God they worship.

Then the picture would change to show Christians celebrating Holy Communion in an Anglican Church. Excerpts of the service would be shown, and an explanation of the meaning of the sacrament would be included. The congregation would be seen taking the bread and the wine and the viewers would be informed that this act of remembering what Christ has done for them is at the heart of Christian worship.

To emphasise this, a short excerpt would then be shown of a march of witness on Good Friday, with the believers following a man carrying a cross. In the background this would be accompanied by a choir singing "The Old Rugged Cross", while the commentator gives a brief explanation.

The scene would then change to an Eastern Orthodox Church early on Easter Sunday morning. It would show candles being lit and the whole Church changing from almost darkness into rows of candle light. The priest would then say "Christ is risen" and the congregation would reply "He is risen indeed". As the commentator explains that Christians worship a risen saviour, in the background would be seen a congregation singing "Christ the Lord is risen today" or another resurrection hymn.

As the offering is being taken and blessed, the commentator then says that Christians believe that "faith without works is dead and so Christians try to help those who are in need." The scene switches to a Salvation Army worker in uniform collecting for their work in the inner cities. It shows people living in cardboard boxes and other places where they can find shelter being given soup by Christian volunteers and being invited to spend the night in a Salvation Army hostel.

Next the programme would focus on Christian Aid and the work that is being done to educate and help people overseas. Scenes would include a person collecting Christian envelopes during Christian Aid Week followed by shots of a drought area of Africa and a project such as an irrigation scheme. This would all be explained by an interview with a Christian Aid worker.

The final section of the programme would include an individual Christian reading a passage from the Bible. The story of Jesus healing Blind Bartimaeus would be a good example and then the individual would pray asking God to help those who are in need. The final shots would show a large group of Christians at prayer asking God to help those who are suffering while the commentator adds that Christianity is about the love of God as shown in Jesus the saviour of the world. Christians respond to this love by worshipping him, praying to him and by attempting to show love to the world where there is much evil and suffering.

Examiner's Comment:

This is a Grade A answer because:

- the candidate has drawn on a wide range of interesting material;
- different traditions within Christianity have been used to good effect;
- it is full of good ideas clearly focused on the task of presenting Christianity in a positive way;
- it clearly shows links between belief and action.

However:

- more technical details of the programme could have been included e.g. overall length and timings for each section.

(b) What might be the benefits of such a programme?

The Benefits of the Programme on "Christianity in Britain Today"

I would hope that this programme would present Christianity in a very positive way. Many people who are my age think of Christians as all being very old and boring. They think of Church as being a very uninteresting place, partly because they do not understand what is going on. Instead of concentrating on long talks or sermons, this programme would be lively and show many young people being involved. Christianity would come over as being cool and attractive. The dancing and music of Spring Harvest would appeal to teenagers and also the idea of helping those in need. Most young people like to do something useful to help rather than sitting around for long periods of time.

Some might criticise what I have planned because they say that it presents a false image of Christianity as they think of Christianity in a quieter way, but I would argue that Christianity should be lively and full of action. Jesus didn't just stay in one place but went out into the countryside and not only preached but he helped people e.g. by healing the sick and going to people who were looked down upon. Christians should be seen helping the people who have no homes or little money. Having believed that Jesus gave his life for you, the challenge of the Christian Faith is to respond by doing something about it. This programme is designed to show not only what Christians believe but how they respond and why. It is about action, although salvation is not earned.

So this programme should present the Christian message simply. It summarises what Christians believe and do and should be interesting for Christians and non-Christians alike. It assumes that viewers know nothing but I believe is interesting even to those who have been members of the Christian Faith for years.

Examiner's comment

This is a Grade A answer because:

- it includes a package of arguments and they are developed logically;
- conclusions are drawn on the main issues and there is recognition that not everyone will approve of the choice of material.

However:

- it does tend to be rather one-sided and doesn't develop arguments concerning tensions which might arise from the material that has been used.

Has the Human Race Progressed?

1 **Discussion starter:** As a class, brainstorm the ways in which you think (a) humanity has progressed throughout history, and (b) humanity has not progressed.

2 What do we mean when we talk about humanity progressing? What point is the story of "Modern Progress" making?

MODERN PROGRESS

When talk of Modern Progress came up one day the Master told of two visitors from a developing country.

He asked about the economic state of their people. One of the callers took offence. But man, he said, we're civilised; we even have a couple of ammunition factories!

[Anthony de Mello, *One Minute Nonsense*, Gujarat Sahitya Prakash, 1992]

A group of students give their viewpoints

"Over the last 150 years humanity has progressed rapidly. We can now fly to the moon and communicate in seconds with anyone in the world. If in 1850 you had declared that it would be possible to clone a sheep you would have been institutionalised. Now the name Dolly holds only that significance. Scientists have also discovered how to halt, and even revise the ageing of cells, bringing immortality within our reach. In a technological sense we have progressed. But not necessarily in the realm of morals." [Marcus, 17]

"Nowadays IVF treatment and abortions are commonplace, and cloning is on the horizon; but do these technological leaps cheapen the value of human life? One day you can grow your own child and abort him/her the next if you wish. When is enough, enough?" [Chris, 15]

"People have become more accepting towards people of different races and nationalities. People are no longer persecuted for being different." [Bethany, 16]

"In the area of ethics we have regressed – not in knowing what is right or wrong, but in our being more willing to put up with wrong things." [Ben, 16]

"The youth, although not following an accepted 'religion', has become more searching. The failure to regularly attend church or mosque is not an indication of decline in spirituality." [Matthew, 16]

"It seems as if we cannot pick up a newspaper nowadays without reading a story of how the teen suicide rate has increased or how teen alcohol and drug abuse is on the rise. But these same newspapers do not write up the stories of ambitious young students starting environmental magazines because they feel that nobody in the government seems to care about, for example, the destruction of the rainforests." [Alicia, 15]

3 Carefully read the viewpoints of this group of students. Then
(a) Choose one you agree with and extend the argument presented.
(b) Choose one you disagree with and write out your own argument.

4 Write your own moral viewpoint article entitled "Has the human race progressed?"

SEG Grade Descriptions

The following descriptions give a general indication of the standards of achievement likely to have been shown by SEG examination candidates awarded particular grades. The descriptions must be interpreted in relation to the content of the syllabus; they are not designed to define that content. In practice, the grade awarded depends on the extent to which the candidate has met the assessment objectives overall. Shortcomings in some aspects of the examination may be balanced by better performance in others. In relation to the religion or religions studied:

Grade F

Candidates demonstrate elementary knowledge and understanding of beliefs, values, and traditions studied and of their impact on adherents and others. They do this through limited use of specialist vocabulary and knowledge, sometimes correctly but not often systematically, and by making simple connections between religion and people's lives. They evaluate responses to issues studied by giving a reason in support of an opinion.

Grade C

Candidates demonstrate, generally with accuracy, a knowledge and understanding of beliefs, values, and traditions studied and of their impact on individuals, societies, and cultures. They do this by using correct specialist vocabulary when questions specifically demand it and by describing accurately and explaining the importance of the key elements of the religion(s) studied. They identify, interpret, and evaluate different responses to issues studied by presenting relevant evidence to support arguments, incorporating references to different points of view, and making reasoned judgements.

Grade A

Candidates demonstrate detailed and comprehensive knowledge and understanding of beliefs, values, and traditions and of their impact on the lives of individuals, societies, and cultures. They do this by consistently using and interpreting a range of specialist vocabulary, drawing out and explaining the meaning and religious significance of the key elements of the religion(s) studied, and explaining, where appropriate, how differences in belief lead to differences of religious response. They support, interpret, and evaluate a variety of responses, recognising the complexity of issues, weighing up opinions, and making reasoned judgements supported by a range of evidence and well-developed arguments.

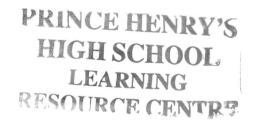

Tips for the SEG Examination

How many religions?

Overall, answers to the whole examination paper may refer to a maximum of three religions, but remember that, in answering each single question you should refer to only one or two religions. You won't be credited with any extra marks for mentioning more than two religions in a single answer, or more than three religions across the whole paper.

If you are referring to two religions in your answer to a question, try to give them equal attention.

Timing

Time is short in the examination. A rough guide is that you should attempt to answer questions equal to one mark per minute. Allowing for reading time, this means that you should spend approximately 10 minutes on Section A, 10 minutes on Section B, and 20 minutes on each of the remaining essay questions.

How to get High Marks

▶ In Part A in particular, try to avoid just giving lists. Include some explanation to show the examiner that you understand what you have included.

▶ Give as many relevant examples as possible, with explanation.

▶ Back up points made by quoting from sacred writings or from the words of modern believers.

▶ Be clear and concise and remain focused on the question.

▶ In Part B in particular, try to include a range of positive responses, actions, and thoughts which are clearly based on religious teachings.

▶ Where possible, include relevant religious technical language.

▶ Include balanced argument with alternative viewpoints, reasons, and evaluation.

▶ Back up arguments with religious teachings and quotations. This will help ensure that your response is appropriate for a Religious Education examination. A sociological or English essay type answer will not obtain the top marks.

Advice on Coursework

Candidates submitting coursework for the SEG examination should provide either a single piece of about 1,000 words, or several separate pieces amounting to that number. The work can be varied in format: e.g. prose, a play, a debate or discussion, a poem, an analysis, or an interview with a visitor. If several pieces of work are provided they must all fit within the chosen "Religion in Action" topic.

Remember:

▶ Supply your coursework in A4 format.

▶ You must not just copy from books. Word-for-word copying is not allowed. However, relevant quotations from books may be included. Make sure you identify them as quotations by using speech marks, and include the source of the quotation – i.e. who said or wrote it, where, and when.

▶ Do not write too much. If your work is much longer than 1,000 words, redraft it and be more precise.

▶ Include a bibliography of resources used.

▶ Be sure that you give a balanced argument followed by a reasoned conclusion. A one-sided discussion of a subject is very unlikely to score many marks.

Sources of Information

Many of the following organisations are registered charities and rely on donations to survive. It is therefore important that you state clearly what information you require and send a stamped addressed envelope with your request for information. Instead of sending multiple copies of a letter, consider sending one copy from a group or a whole class.

CHRISTIANITY
Catholic Education Service,
38-40 Eccleston Square, London SW1P 1LT

Church of England Enquiries Centre,
Church House, Great Smith Street,
Westminster, London SW1P 3NZ
020 7222 9011

Methodist Church,
25 Marylebone Road, London NW1 5JR
020 7486 5502

Orthodox Church Information Service,
64 Prebend Gardens, London W6 0XY

The Religious Society of Friends (Quakers),
Friends House, Euston Road, London NW1 2BJ

HINDUISM
Hinduism Today on line: www.hinduismtoday.com
This popular Hindu magazine includes up-to-date articles on news events.

ISLAM
Islamic Consultancy and Information Service,
PO Box 2842, London W6 9ZH
020 8748 24242

Islamic Foundation Publications Unit,
Unit 9, The Old Dunlop Factory,
62 Evington Valley Road, Leicester LE5 5LJ
01533 734860

Muslim Education Trust,
130 Stroud Green Road, London N4 3RZ
020 7281 3457

Muslim Information Service,
233 Seven Sisters Road, London N4 2DA

JUDAISM
Board of Deputies of British Jews,
Woburn House, Upper Woburn Place,
London WC1H 0EP

Jewish Education Bureau,
8 Westcombe Avenue, Leeds LS8 2BS

Office of the Chief Rabbi,
Adler House, Tavistock Square,
London WC1H 9HN

Two websites to visit for information on Kashrut are:
http://baptist1.com/judaism/kashrut.htm
http://isaac.exploratorium.edu/bluethread/kashrut/discussion.html

SIKHISM
http://sikhnet.com

http://www.sikhmall.com/sandeep/khalsavideo.html

http://www.sikh-institute.org/

http://www.sikhspirit.com/

http://photon.bu.edu/~rajwi/sikhism/mansukh1.html

There is an English translation of the Guru Granth Sahib on line: www.sikhs.org/english/frame

ISSUES OF LIFE AND DEATH
EXIT (Voluntary Euthanasia Society),
13 Prince of Wales Terrace, London W8 3PG
020 7937 7770

LIFE (anti-abortion campaign),
1a Newbold Terrace, Leamington Spa CV32 4EA
01926 421587

National Abortion Campaign,
The Print House, 18 Ashwin Street, London E8 3DL
020 7923 4976

Society for the Protection of the Unborn Child,
7 Tufton Street, London SW1P 3QN
020 7222 5845

THE ENVIRONMENT
Animal Aid,
7 Castle Street, Tonbridge, Kent TN9 1BH

Animal Christian Concern,
46 St Margaret's Road, Horsforth, Leeds LS18 5BG
0113 258 3517

Christian Ecology Group,
58 Quest Hills Road, Malvern,
Worcestershire WR14 1RW

Earthkind,
Humane Education Centre, Bounds Green Road,
London N22 4EU

Friends of the Earth,
26-28 Underwood Street, London N1 7JQ
020 7490 1555

Greenpeace UK,
Canonbury Villas, London N1 2PN
Tel.: 020 7865 8100; Fax: 020 7865 8200
e-mail: gp-info@uk.greenpeace.org

The Lifestyle Movement,
Manor Farm, Little Gidding, Huntingdon PE17 5RJ

World Wide Fund for Nature,
Education Department, Weyside Park, Godalming,
Surrey GU7 1XR

WEALTH AND POVERTY
CAFOD (Catholic Agency for Overseas Development),
Romero Close, Stockwell Road, London SW9 9TY
020 7733 7900

Christian Aid (overseas and development work),
PO Box 100, London SE1 7RT
020 7620 4444

Church Action on Poverty,
Central Buildings, Oldham Street,
Manchester M1 1JT

Islamic Relief,
151B Park Road, London NW8 7HT
Tel.: 020 7722 0039; Fax: 020 7722 3228
E-mail: irww@compuserve.com

Jubilee 2000 - Debt Cancellation,
Globalchange.com/debtrelief.htm

Muslim Aid,
Dept. FA52, PO Box 3, London N7 8LR
www.muslimaid.org

Tear Fund,
11 Station Road, Teddington,
Middlesex TW11 9AA
020 8977 9144

World Vision (development and aid),
599 Avebury Boulevard, Milton Keynes,
Bucks MK9 3PG
01908 841000

PREJUDICE
Commission for Racial Equality,
10-12 Allington House, London SW1E 5EH

RELATIONSHIPS

For Marriage and Divorce Statistics:

Office for National Statistics,
Room 2300, Segensworth Road, Titchfield, Fareham,
Hants PO15 5RR

Lesbian and Gay Christians,
Oxford House, Derbyshire Street,
London E2 6HG
www://members.aol.com/lgcm

Relate,
Herbert Gray College, Little Church Street,
Rugby CV21 3AP

WAR AND PEACE

Amnesty International,
99-119 Rosebery Avenue, London EC1R 4RE
020 7814 6200

Christian CND,
St Mary's Church, Bramall Lane, Sheffield S2 4QZ
0114 273 9047

CND (Campaign for Nuclear Disarmament),
22-24 Underwood Street, London N1 7JG

Quaker Peace and Service,
Friends House, Euston Road, London NW1 2BJ

War Child,
7-12 Greenland Street, London NW1 0ND
Tel.: 020 7916 9276; Fax: 020 7916 9280
e-mail: mir@warchild.demon.co.uk

RELIGION AND SCIENCE

Christians in Science,
Atholl Centre, Atholl Road, Pitlochry, Perthshire PH16 5BX
01796 473044